Eat Like a Greek

Eat Like a Greek

100 Quick, Easy, Delicious Recipes

Marina Georgallides

hamlyn

To my beloved *yiayiá* (grandma), a golden woman
στην αγαπημένη μου Γιαγιά, μια χρυσή γυναίκα

First published in Great Britain in 2026 by Hamlyn,
an imprint of Octopus Publishing Group Ltd,
Carmelite House, 50 Victoria Embankment,
London EC4Y 0DZ
www.octopusbooks.co.uk

An Hachette UK Company
www.hachette.co.uk

The authorized representative in the EEA is Hachette Ireland, 8 Castlecourt Centre, Dublin 15, D15 XTP3, Ireland (email: info@hbgi.ie)

Text copyright © Marina Georgallides 2026

Distributed in the US by Hachette Book Group, 1290 Avenue of the Americas, 4th and 5th Floors, New York, NY 10104
Distributed in Canada by Canadian Manda Group, 664 Annette St, Toronto, Ontario, Canada M6S 2C8

All rights reserved. No part of this work may be reproduced or utilized in any form or by any means, electronic or mechanical, including photocopying, recording or by any information storage and retrieval system, without the prior written permission of the publisher.

Marina Georgallides asserts the moral right to be identified as the author of this work.

ISBN: 9780600639299
eISBN: 9780600639305

A CIP catalogue record for this book is available from the British Library.

Printed and bound in China.

10 9 8 7 6 5 4 3 2 1

Publisher: **Kate Fox**
Art Director: **Juliette Norsworthy**
Senior Editor: **Leanne Bryan**
Photographer: **Andrew Burton**
Food Stylist: **Emily Jonzen**
Props Stylist: **Max Robinson**
Cover Designer & Illustrator: **Luke Bird**
Production Controllers: **Lucy Carter & Nic Jones**

Additional picture credits

iStock: Alabady 60br, 63, Aleksei Gur 33cr, 161, 222ar, 230, Alex-White 90ar, Anna Shelkova 138, 155, beinluck 222al, Creation of icons and illustrations 90, 110, Ekaterina Buravleva 118ar, 125, EZEEproject 153, 154bl, 200, Gabriel Onat 188bl, Ganna Galata 117, 189, hirose 118cl, 135, Ivan Shchytko 32bl, 60, Kolonko 154cl, 186, 209, Mariia Levchenko 13ar, 27, 145, MartaJonina 172, Nataliia Omelchenko 13al, oleg7799 98, 212, ???bl, setory 12cr, 22, 56, 68cr, 119, 154br, 223cr, sudhaben sachapara 105, Sylfida 181, 188br, ulimi 32c, 69br, 90ar (bg), 90cr, 118br, 154cr, vectorartnow 68cl, Victor Metelskiy 47, 118 above left, 148.

Cookery notes

Standard level spoon measurements are used in all recipes.

1 tablespoon = one 15ml spoon
1 teaspoon = one 5ml spoon

Pints are UK volumes (20fl oz).

Ovens should be preheated to the specific temperature. For Centigrade if using a conventional, not fan-assisted, oven, increase the stated temperature by 20°C.

Some recipes give the option of using an air fryer. Make sure the air fryer is preheated before cooking and use a liner in the tray or basket when adding liquids such as oils or marinades.

Root vegetables such as potatoes, onions, garlic and carrots are peeled unless otherwise stated.

Contents

WELCOME **6**
DIPS LIKE A GREEK **12**
MEZZE LIKE A GREEK **32**
SALADS LIKE A GREEK **68**
EVERYDAY DINNERS LIKE A GREEK **90**
FEAST LIKE A GREEK **118**
SHARE LIKE A GREEK **154**
SWEET TREATS LIKE A GREEK **188**
GREEK STAPLES **222**
INDEX **234**
UK/US TERMS **238**
ACKNOWLEDGEMENTS **239**
ABOUT THE AUTHOR **240**

Welcome

Whether you're already a fan of my recipes or you've never heard of me before, I want to give you the warmest welcome. I'm Marina, known as @chefmarinie on social media, and if there's one thing you should know about me as you acquaint yourself with this book is just how much I love food. You might be wondering: isn't that a prerequisite for anyone writing a cookbook? And the answer is: yes, absolutely. But the love I'm talking about is the kind where, no matter how sleep-deprived and exhausted I am, the prospect of breakfast will always get me out of bed; the kind where I'll be eating said breakfast while also thinking about my next meal of the day. No matter the circumstances, this love drives me into the kitchen and motivates me to spend hours after a long day at work as well as all my free time at the weekend, cooking and sharing my creations on the internet. Very few things in life bring me as much joy.

Food is synonymous with the act of togetherness.

As a Greek Cypriot, born in Cyprus and raised in London, the idea of connection through food and the many meanings it carries for me is what foregrounds *Eat Like a Greek*. Connection to my heritage; connection to friends and long-distance family and how food is synonymous with the act of togetherness; and connection to an online community to whom I owe my deepest gratitude.

My love of food began in childhood. I cherish the memories of watching my force-to-be-reckoned-with *yiayiá* (grandma) prepare all sorts of incredible Greek food. She was a dynamic woman, and nothing ever phased or stopped her, however seemingly complicated or labour-intensive the dish. My siblings and I would always come home to find her preparing something absolutely delicious. Whether she was on her feet for hours, carefully crafting perfectly wrapped *dolmadákia*, or – despite her arthritis – kneading dough by hand for *koulourákia*,

flaoúnes, elaiopitákia and other baked treats, her dedication to feeding our family something new every day, and the delight she took from our response to it, has been the source of my inspiration and sense of connection to my heritage.

From living with my two best friends in my final year of university, I soon realized the joy I derive from making food for other people. It began with baking the odd Victoria sponge or lemon and poppyseed cake on days where I wanted to do anything but study, and led to promises of baking future wedding cakes. Years later that promise became a reality, and I found myself transporting a four-tier hummingbird cake and six traybakes in a Deliveroo-style insulated delivery bag across London. I had never baked a wedding cake before and, despite having been displeased with my every previous attempt at buttercream, somehow I managed to make it perfectly for the day itself. Watching my bestie and her husband cut through the cake on their special day (and seeing it stay intact) meant the world to me, and made me realize that my dedication to showing love through food knows no bounds.

I see the warmth and hospitality I learned from my *yiayiá* as the thing that's allowed me to stay connected with friends from different periods of my life. London – the city I love and where I've lived for most of my life – is often a place of toing and froing, with little time to pause and convene. But if there's one thing that gets people to trek from one end of the city to the other it is the lure of a damn good dinner party. For me, putting on a spread for friends and family is the perfect way to celebrate birthdays and special occasions. Spending hours preparing food – sometimes even days before – is a worthy pursuit in my eyes because it means bringing together the people I love and care about through relishing a shared experience. Consider this book an extension of that!

My dedication to showing love through food knows no bounds.

My journey into food content creation began in earnest during a time when, like many of us, I was filling the void of lockdown with a passion project. I challenged myself to post a recipe every single day for a month. The act of documenting and sharing my food creations on the internet spurred me on to cook more and become better at it. Before I knew it, I was connecting with other like-minded foodies and became immersed in an online community that I would characterize as inspiring and supportive. I never anticipated the response – the thousands of people commenting, saving and recreating those recipes – and I'm endlessly grateful for the platform it's afforded me and the links I've forged as a result.

Balancing full-time work alongside making recipes for the internet hasn't been an easy feat. It's always been a priority for me to develop recipes that are accessible, convenient and fit into my busy schedule. You'll notice that some of the recipes in this cookbook have been adapted or simplified to meet this need and are designed to be weeknight staples.

About the book

Eat Like a Greek is as much rooted in tradition as it is a celebration of innovative Greek recipes fit for ease and convenience. Whether it's recreating a traditional dish in the best possible way or finding ingenious ways to reimagine it, as the title suggests, the key is in 'like'. It's about celebrating the breadth and simplicity of Greek food and proving just how easy it can be to recreate the classic dishes we all know and love using fresh ingredients and simple cooking methods. Take it from all the people who have (re)discovered and (re)created their all-time favourite Greek dishes through my recipes and praised them for their ease.

Eat Like a Greek is about celebrating the breadth and simplicity of Greek food.

In *Eat Like a Greek*, you'll find everything from the hits from my channel to the classics as well as some lesser-known dishes that I grew up eating – dips, salads, breads, hearty meals, desserts and much more. Every recipe celebrates Greek cuisine and its representation of Greek culture – whether that's through recipes fit to feed a gathering or share with loved ones, traditional meals made more simply or in using copious amounts of extra virgin olive oil and lemon juice wherever possible!

You'll find that every chapter in *Eat Like a Greek* serves a particular desire or need. If you're anything like me and love to host, you'll know that having a repertoire of quick and delicious recipes that you can rely on without having to think about is vital. In Dips and Mezze Like a Greek, I share some of the most iconic recipes that Greek cuisine is known for – like *saganáki* and *kalamári* – sensational appetizers that use minimal ingredients, and all of the classic dips which you can easily recreate at home and make even better. But not all Greek recipes are quick and easy. So, I've created a chapter dedicated to weeknight meals – Everyday Dinners Like a Greek contains convenient alternatives to the hearty, comforting dishes I grew up eating. You'll love just how easy they are, and I guarantee you'll want them as go-to meals on busy weeknights.

While I appreciate ease and convenience in cooking, creating shareable centrepiece dishes for gatherings is as much a worthwhile labour of love as it is a facet of Greek culture, with bringing family and friends together through food at the heart. In Feast Like a Greek, you'll find those low-and-slow dishes that are worth every bit of effort and are best enjoyed at special occasions or for large crowds. My personal favourite is *kléftiko* (see page 150) – lamb marinated in lots of gorgeous herbs and garlic and slow-cooked until perfectly tender.

As well as hosting and putting on a spread, sharing baked treats – especially when visiting friends and family – is a huge part of what I associate with Greek culture as it's common to show up with an edible treat in hand. I usually package any shareable goods into little parcels and drop them off at friends, especially during festive celebrations, such as Christmas, New Year and Easter. At these times, treats like *koulourákia* (Greek Easter cookies, page 174) and *kourabiedés* (buttery shortbread biscuits that are traditionally baked during Christmas, page 187), are made in large batches and handed out as tokens of appreciation. You'll find these recipes and so many other treats, both sweet and savoury, in this book.

For the less transportable but equally divine treats, I've dedicated a whole section to hearty desserts featuring my one true love: *siropiastá* (meaning syrup-soaked), a category of Greek desserts that are utterly delicious. Sweet Treats Like a Greek features the very best, from my all-time favourites *lemonópita* and *portokalópita* (lemon and orange filo cakes, see pages 195–6), to lesser-known ones such as *indokaridópita* (coconut cake, page 208) and *amygdalópita* (almond cake, page 207). Besides these, you'll also find some yogurt-based desserts that are healthy-ish (at least a lot healthier than anything syrup-soaked!) as well as a no-bake Greek take on halva (see page 220) that requires minimal ingredients.

Before you dive into any of these chapters, I'd like to take a moment to say how much I appreciate you being here. My hope is that you enjoy eating like a Greek just as much as I do!

Dips

Gr

1. Dip

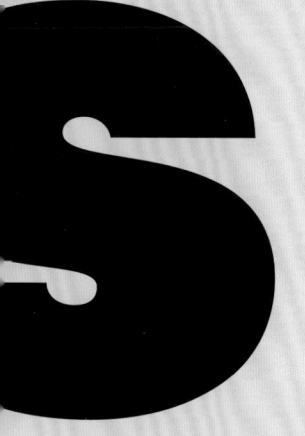

Nobody does dips quite like the Greek-Cypriots! There are so many to choose from, but here are some of my favourites, including **tyrokaftéri** – a red pepper and feta dip that's gorgeously creamy, garlicky and spicy – and **skordaliá** – a simple garlicky potato dip whipped to creamy perfection. Of course, I had to have my **tzatziki** recipe here, as it's my absolute favourite and rated by my friends and family as the best one out there. Beyond the classics, you'll find equally delicious dips that take inspiration from traditional ones. If you love feta as much I do, then you're guaranteed to love my **courgette feta dip** that's creamy, herby and tangy all at once, or, for a fuss-free option, try **sweet and spicy baked feta topped with chilli crisp and honey**. Whatever the occasion, grab some pitta or flatbread and get dipping!

NTIP FÉTAS KOLOKYTHIOÚ

Courgette Feta Dip

If you love feta as much as I do, I'm certain this dip will be a winner: think tzatziki made with courgette instead of cucumber, and with feta cheese as well as yogurt. The result is this creamy, tangy, silken dip that will leave you wanting more with every mouthful. The sweetness of the courgette complements the sharp creaminess of the feta, and the lemon juice brightens it all.

SERVES 4

1 courgette, roughly chopped

3 tablespoons extra virgin olive oil

200g (7oz) feta cheese

100g (3½oz) Greek yogurt (10% fat)

1 garlic clove, grated or crushed

handful of dill fronds, finely chopped

½ lemon, juiced

salt to taste

1 Preheat the oven to 180°C fan (400°F), Gas Mark 6 and line a large baking tray with baking paper. Slice the courgette into rounds roughly 5mm (¼ inch) thick. Place the slices on the baking tray and drizzle with 2 tablespoons of the olive oil. Toss to coat them evenly in the oil then bake for 25–30 minutes, until soft.

2 Transfer the courgette to a serving bowl and add the feta and yogurt. Mash with a fork to a smooth consistency, mixing for about 2 minutes to ensure everything is combined. Add the garlic, dill, lemon juice and remaining oil and continue mixing until well incorporated. Check the seasoning and add salt to taste.

3 Serve the dip at room temperature or chilled – it will keep until the next day covered and stored in the fridge. Enjoy with flatbread (see page 57) or pitta bread (see pages 58–60).

AIR FRYER Another way to cook the chopped courgette is to place it in an air fryer and coat in a tablespoon of olive oil and the pinch of salt. Air-fry for 12 minutes at 180°C (350°F), turning halfway through.

HOÚMOUS

Hummus

My version of hummus includes garlic and lemon, of course. And although this version isn't traditional in the sense that it uses canned chickpeas instead of soaking and boiling dried ones beforehand, it's far quicker and certainly just as delicious – and better than any shop-bought one. It's as simple as chucking everything into a food processor and blitzing until perfectly creamy. I use a pinch of lemon zest as well as the juice for zing, and a hint of ground cumin and smoked paprika, which add a warming undertone.

SERVES 6

400g (14oz) can chickpeas, drained and rinsed

40g (1½oz) tahini

100ml (3½fl oz) hot water

zest and juice of ½ lemon

1 garlic clove

½ teaspoon ground cumin

½ teaspoon smoked paprika

2 tablespoons extra virgin olive oil, plus extra for drizzling

salt to taste

1 Put the drained chickpeas, tahini and hot water into a food processor and blitz for 30 seconds until a paste forms. Then add the lemon zest and juice, garlic and spices and blitz again. With the motor still running, slowly pour the oil through the tube. After another minute, the consistency will be thick and creamy.

2 Check the seasoning and add salt to taste. Carefully pour the hummus into a serving bowl and refrigerate for an hour before serving – this way it firms up to the perfect consistency for dipping.

3 Once the hummus is ready, drizzle with extra olive oil and enjoy with flatbread (see page 57) or pitta bread (see pages 58–60). Stored in an airtight container in the fridge, this hummus will keep for 3 days.

TYROKAFTÉRI

Spicy Feta Dip

Tyrokaftéri has a special place in my heart: it's what kicked off my *Eat Like a Greek* series on social media. Its name aptly translates into English as 'spicy cheese', perfectly describing its punchy flavour profile. The dip is made from whipped feta with roasted red peppers, garlic and olive oil, and it's seasoned with dried chilli flakes and oregano. It's creamy, tangy, a little spicy and beautifully rich without being heavy for an appetizer. I love serving this with warm pitta (see pages 58–60) or my signature chicken gyros (see page 133).

SERVES 4

1 pointed red pepper, stem and seeds removed, cut into chunks

2 tablespoons extra virgin olive oil

200g (7oz) feta cheese

2 garlic cloves

2 teaspoons red wine vinegar

½ teaspoon chilli flakes

½ teaspoon dried oregano

2 tablespoons water

salt to taste

1 Preheat the oven to 180°C fan (400°F), Gas Mark 6 and line a baking tray with baking paper. Place the pepper chunks on the tray and drizzle with a tablespoon of olive oil. Toss to coat them evenly in the oil then roast for 20–25 minutes, until softened and charred slightly.

2 Transfer the cooked peppers to a blender or food processor along with the rest of the ingredients and blitz for 1–2 minutes until a smooth paste forms. Check the seasoning and add salt to taste.

3 Spoon the dip into a serving bowl. It will still be warm at this point, and I would recommend placing it in the fridge for at least 30 minutes before serving. Enjoy with flatbread (see page 57) or pitta bread (see pages 58–60).

AIR FRYER If you're pressed for time, the red pepper chunks can be roasted in an air fryer. Simply add them to your air-fryer tray, coat in 1 tablespoon of olive oil, and air-fry at 180°C (350°F) for 10–12 minutes until they are charred.

PIKÁNTIKO NTIP FÉTAS MELIOU

Spicy Honey Feta Dip

I simply love the combination of feta, chilli oil, honey and walnuts: it's salty, spicy, sweet and crunchy. Although not traditionally Greek, this dip is inspired by the chilli-flavoured feta dip *tyrokaftéri* (see page 20). It requires very little preparation other than chopping up the walnuts – making it perfect for whipping up when you have little time on your hands.

SERVES 4

1 tablespoon extra virgin olive oil

200g (7oz) block feta cheese, patted dry with kitchen paper

2 teaspoons chilli crisp

2 teaspoons runny honey

30g (1oz) walnuts, chopped

1 Preheat the oven to 180°C fan (400°F), Gas Mark 6 and grease a small baking dish with the oil. Place the block of feta in the middle and top it with the chilli crisp, honey and walnuts. Bake for 20 minutes, or until the walnuts are golden brown and the feta has softened.

2 Using a fork, roughly mash up the feta and mix it with the oil, chilli and walnuts to a smooth consistency. Serve the dip still warm with crackers or pitta bread (see pages 58–60). It will keep in the fridge for a day if you don't end up eating it all in one sitting. You will need to reheat it just enough to soften the feta.

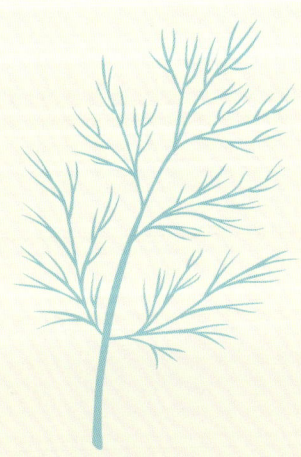

Tzatziki

This wouldn't be a Greek cookbook without tzatziki, and this is one of my signature recipes. I boast that it's the best homemade tzatziki because all my friends and family who have tried it boldly claim that it's better than any they have had in Greece which, for me, is the highest praise. The trick to a perfect creamy consistency is to grate the cucumbers and remove the excess liquid. I prefer Lebanese cucumbers here, because they're sweeter and crunchier than regular ones. My own spin on this classic dip is to add dried oregano as well as dried mint and finely chopped fresh dill, giving the tzatziki an even fresher taste than usual that packs a punch with every mouthful. Likewise, pink Himalayan salt also gives depth.

SERVES 4–6

4 baby or Lebanese cucumbers

500g (1lb 2oz) Greek yogurt (10% fat)

40g (1½oz) dill fronds

2 teaspoons dried mint

2 teaspoons dried oregano

2 garlic cloves, grated or crushed

2 tablespoons extra virgin olive oil, plus extra for drizzling

juice of 1 lemon

salt to taste (I use about 1 heaped teaspoon pink Himalayan salt)

pinch of smoked paprika, to serve

1 Trim off both ends of the cucumbers and grate them. Place them on a clean muslin cloth or tea towel and wrap them up and squeeze really hard to remove all the excess liquid. Once drained, transfer the grated cucumber to a large mixing bowl and add the Greek yogurt.

2 Finely chop the dill. I like to do this by removing the fronds from the stem and finely slicing this first before finely chopping the fronds. Add to the bowl along with the dried herbs, garlic, extra virgin olive oil, lemon juice and salt. Give everything a very good mix to combine. Check the taste and add more of any of the ingredients to your liking.

3 Once combined, transfer the tzatziki to a serving bowl and drizzle a little more olive oil on top and add a light dusting of paprika for colour. Enjoy this with warm pitta bread (see pages 58–60), crisps or anything you can dip with.

NTIP TACHÍNI

Tahini Dip

This Greek-style tahini is everything you would want from a dip – and it's so much more than the plain tahini from a jar. There's a healthy amount of garlic and lemon juice to complement the nutty flavour of the tahini. I whip up this dip with a handheld blender until the texture is perfectly thick and creamy, and I love to serve it chilled as the texture becomes even richer and more dippable. It can also be served right after it's been prepared – it will be more liquid but is great for drizzling. It pairs beautifully with toasted pitta (see pages 58–60) or flatbread (see page 57), or with stuffed vine leaves (see page 55), which is my favourite way to enjoy this dip.

SERVES 4–6

250g (9oz) tahini
250ml (9fl oz) lukewarm water
juice of 2½ lemons
2 garlic cloves, grated
salt to taste
chopped parsley, to garnish (optional)

1 Add all the ingredients to a large bowl, starting with the tahini. Blitz using a handheld blender for 2 minutes, or until the water and lemon juice emulsify and the tahini becomes smooth. Taste: you may want to adjust the salt or acidity to your preference – use the amounts listed as a guide.

2 Transfer the dip to a sealable container and refrigerate for 1 hour to firm up before serving sprinkled with chopped parsley, if liked. Alternatively, you can serve it straight away if you prefer a runnier consistency. Sealed, the dip will keep for up to 3 days in the fridge.

TOP TIP My preference when it comes to brands of tahini is Cypressa because it's less runny than others. You could also replace the tahini with sesame paste – it is thicker than tahini, so your dip may not need chilling before serving.

MELITZÁNOSALÁTA

Aubergine Dip

This aromatic herby dip is made from aubergines and red pepper that are softened by roasting, which adds a sweet and chargrilled flavour as well as a vibrant colour. Garlic, extra virgin olive oil and white wine vinegar are blitzed to form a creamy and bright dressing which is combined with the roasted veg. Think of *melitzánosaláta* as a chunkier and fresher-tasting version of baba ghanoush!

SERVES 4

2 aubergines

2 tablespoons extra virgin olive oil, plus an extra drizzle for roasting

1 pointed red pepper, halved lengthways, stem and seeds removed

2 tablespoons white wine vinegar

3 garlic cloves

salt to taste

To garnish

2 spring onions, finely chopped

15g (½oz) parsley, finely chopped

1 Preheat the oven to 180°C fan (400°F), Gas Mark 6 and line a baking tray with baking paper. Pierce the aubergines with a fork (this allows steam to escape during the cooking process and ensures that they cook evenly). Place them on the tray, rub with a light drizzle of extra virgin olive oil and season with a sprinkle of salt. Bake for 45–50 minutes, or until the aubergines have softened and are slightly charred on top. About halfway through the cooking time, add the pepper halves to the baking tray.

2 Once both veg have softened and charred slightly, transfer them to a bowl, cover with clingfilm and leave them to cool for 30 minutes. Trapping in the moisture will make it easier to peel off their skin.

3 Meanwhile, add the oil, vinegar, garlic and salt to a blender or food processor and blitz until a smooth dressing has formed.

4 Peel off the skins from the peppers and scoop the flesh from the aubergines. Finely chop the soft flesh to a mushy consistency. Add this to a serving bowl, pour in the dressing and mix until well combined.

5 Sprinkle the *melitzánosaláta* with finely chopped spring onion and parsley. Enjoy with flatbread (see page 57) or pitta bread (see pages 58–60).

NTIP KRITINOU BIZELIOU

Split Pea Dip

Rich and velvety fava dip (*Ntip fávas*) is the sexy Greek counterpart of hummus and is served in most tavernas in Greece. The special type of fava beans used to make this dip are cultivated only on the island of Santorini, so the variation I've shared here uses the more widely available yellow split peas, which make an equally delicious dip.

SERVES 4

- 2 tablespoons extra virgin olive oil, plus extra for drizzling
- 1 red onion, chopped
- 3 garlic cloves, crushed or grated
- 220g (8oz) dried yellow split peas
- 1 teaspoon dried thyme (for preference, or use fresh thyme leaves)
- 2 bay leaves
- 1 vegetable stock cube, dissolved in 720ml (scant 1⅓ pints) hot water
- juice of 1 lemon
- salt to taste
- sprinkle of smoked paprika, to serve

1 Pour the oil into a saucepan and place over a medium heat. After 1 minute, add the onion and garlic and sauté for 2–3 minutes until they soften and become fragrant. Add the yellow split peas, thyme, bay leaves and prepared stock. Stir to combine and leave to simmer for 25 minutes, stirring regularly, or until the stock has reduced and the split peas have mostly softened. Don't worry if they still have some 'bite' as everything will be blended.

2 Take the pan off the heat and remove the bay leaves. Carefully pour the contents into a food processor, add the lemon juice and blitz for about 1 minute until the dip is thick and creamy. Taste, and add salt as needed.

3 Transfer to a bowl and serve the dip either warm or at room temperature with a drizzle of olive oil and a light sprinkle of paprika on top. Enjoy with flatbread (see page 57) or pitta bread (see pages 58–60). You can also store the dip in the fridge in an airtight container and eat within 2 days.

SKORDALIÁ

Garlicky Potato Dip

Skordaliá is a staple feature of any Greek mezze spread. Made from just a few ingredients, the simple flavour combination of white wine vinegar, garlic and good-quality extra virgin olive oil combined with puréed potato is not to be underestimated. For a silky-smooth consistency, I recommend blitzing the dip in a food processor, but you can also achieve a perfectly dippable texture just by mashing the ingredients by hand. Serve as a dip with flatbread (see page 57), pitta (see pages 58–60) or as a side with grilled meat or fish.

SERVES 4–6

650–700g (1lb 7–9oz) floury white potatoes, peeled and cut into even-sized pieces

3 garlic cloves

generous 2 tablespoons white wine vinegar

generous 3 tablespoons extra virgin olive oil, plus extra to serve

2 spring onions, chopped

parsley, finely chopped

salt to taste (I used about 2 teaspoons)

1 Put the potatoes in a saucepan with just enough water to cover. Add a sprinkle of salt and place the pan over a medium heat. Boil for 20–25 minutes until the potatoes are fork tender. Drain and leave them in a colander for at least 10 minutes to cool and dry.

2 Once the potatoes have cooled, transfer them to a food processor along with the garlic, vinegar, olive oil and salt. Blitz for a minute to a smooth and creamy purée. Blitz again for another minute if necessary to smooth out any lumps. Alternatively, if you don't have a food processor, simply put the cooled potatoes in a large bowl with the same ingredients and mash by hand until you achieve a smooth consistency. This will take a few more minutes.

3 Serve the *skordaliá* with a drizzle of olive oil on top, and sprinkle with chopped spring onions and parsley. You can store it in the fridge in an airtight container and eat within 2 days.

TARAMASALÁTA

Taramasalata

This classic Greek dip is perfect for serving as part of a mezze spread. It's made from pressed cod roe and bread, whipped to a gorgeously creamy consistency with oil and lemon juice, which adds its tang to the umami-rich cod roe. Most taramasalata that is sold in shops is dyed pink, but when prepared at home with high-quality pressed cod roe (which you can find in cans in bigger supermarkets), the colour is paler and a lot more subtle. Using the recipe below, you'll see just how easy and even more delicious it is to make taramasalata yourself.

SERVES 6–8

1 shallot, roughly chopped

300ml (10fl oz) water

200g (7oz) white baguette, cut into small chunks

200g (7oz) pressed cod roe

juice of 2 lemons

generous 3 tablespoons extra virgin olive oil, plus extra for drizzling

5 tablespoons sunflower oil

salt to taste

1 Put the chopped shallot in a small bowl and submerge under 100ml (3½fl oz) of the measured water. Set aside for 15 minutes to soften the sharpness of the raw shallot.

2 Meanwhile, put the baguette chunks in a large bowl. Pour over the remaining water and allow the bread to fully absorb it – after about 20 seconds the crusts will soften and the soft crumb in the middle will be slightly soggy. Transfer to a food processor along with the drained chopped shallot. Blitz on a high speed for 1 minute until a paste forms.

3 Add the pressed cod roe and blitz for another minute.

4 Mix the lemon juice and oils in a jug and, with the motor still running, slowly pour in this liquid through the tube of the food processor. Season with salt to taste and continue blitzing until the taramasalata has emulsified and the consistency is completely smooth.

5 Transfer the taramasalata to a serving bowl, drizzle with extra virgin olive oil and enjoy with flatbread (see page 57) or pitta bread (see pages 58–60). Stored in an airtight container in the fridge it will keep for 3 days.

2. Mez

From cheesy delights to pillowy soft breads, this chapter is where you'll find those classic small plates traditionally served in Greek tavernas, as well as other appetizers that are perfect for nibbling on. Fancy making a small plate in less than 20 minutes? Try my **saganáki**, the famous pan-fried cheese dish, made perfectly crispy with a shredded kataïfi coating. Or there's **ravasáki**, a filo-wrapped block of feta, pan-fried to make a gorgeously crunchy parcel with a gooey centre. Something to dunk into dips? Let me introduce you to the best **flatbreads** made with just a handful of ingredients. I've also included a traditional tear-and-share **Cypriot village bread** that's gorgeously aromatic with spices. Beyond breads, you'll find three types of herby fritters that really showcase the fresh flavours of Greek cuisine with their generous use of mint and dill: choose from **tomato fritters**, **crispy courgette fritters** or oven-baked **chickpea patties**. To take your mezze spread to the next level, you must try my **eliés tsakistés** – a Cypriot-style way of dressing green olives in lots of garlic, lemon juice and crushed coriander seeds.

ELIÉS TSAKISTÉS

Marinated Green Olives

Eliés tsakistés translates as 'cracked green olives', referring to the Cypriot custom of cracking open and marinating fresh green olives in a gorgeous garlicky-lemony brine. They're an absolute flavour bomb when eaten on their own, which is what I tend to do whenever I'm in Cyprus. But they're also delicious when served as part of a mezze spread. The traditional way of preparing them requires harvesting fresh green olives, but here I'm using shop-bought olives in brine. It comes together in just a few minutes, making it an excellent component of any mezze spread. The key to making the olives pack a punch is to add lots of garlic, more lemon juice than you think and crushed coriander seeds.

SERVES 4

200g (7oz) pitted green olives in brine, drained

1 tablespoon coriander seeds, roughly crushed using a pestle and mortar

3 garlic cloves, crushed

1½ lemons, 1 juiced and ½ thinly sliced

2 tablespoons extra virgin olive oil

1 Place the drained olives in a bowl with the crushed coriander seeds and garlic.

2 Pour the lemon juice over the olives, along with the oil. Cut the lemon slices into quarters and add to the olives.

3 Mix everything together until the olives are evenly coated. Cover and store in the fridge for at least a day (and up to a week) so that the pungency of the garlic softens. Enjoy as an appetizer.

TOP TIP Don't throw away that delicious marinade! Instead, use it as a dip for pitta bread (see pages 58–60).

TOMATOKEFTÉDES

Tomato Fritters

In Greek the word *keftédes* can mean fritters or patties, and these tomato fritters are aromatic and herby, enriched with mint, basil and parsley, just three of the many herbs you find growing wild in Greece. The trick to making them delicious is to use both chopped and grated tomatoes in the batter, which cooks to a crisp and golden crust and adds more texture and bite to the fritters. Not only are *tomatokeftédes* quick to whip up, but they're also naturally vegan.

SERVES 4

3 beef tomatoes (about 650g/1lb 7oz), cored and halved

1 courgette (about 250g/9oz), trimmed

325g (11½oz) plain flour

1½ teaspoons baking powder

4 spring onions, finely chopped

15g (½oz) mint leaves, chopped

15g (½oz) basil leaves, chopped

15g (½oz) parsley, chopped

2 teaspoons dried oregano

1 tablespoon extra virgin olive oil

250ml (9fl oz) vegetable or sunflower oil, for frying

salt and pepper

1 Cut half the tomatoes into quarters. Set aside. Cut the remaining tomatoes in half and grate them coarsely (discard the skins), then set them aside. Using the same grater, grate the courgette and set this aside too.

2 Sift the flour and baking powder into a large mixing bowl and stir to blend. Create a well in the middle and add both the grated and the chopped tomatoes.

3 Add the chopped spring onions and fresh herbs to the mixture, along with the grated courgette, dried oregano, seasoning and extra virgin olive oil.

4 Using your hands or a wooden spoon, gently stir to combine the ingredients until the flour is fully incorporated and a batter forms.

5 Pour the vegetable oil into a large frying pan and place over a medium heat. Leave the oil to heat up for about 2 minutes. You can test the temperature by sticking the tip of a wooden spoon in the pan and seeing if the oil bubbles up around it. Once the oil is hot enough, add a tablespoon of the batter and, depending on how large your frying pan is, repeat this 7 or 8 times. You want to leave a gap between the fritters to allow them to cook evenly and become golden brown, so it's best to fry them in batches.

6 Fry the fritters for 2–3 minutes on each side until they become crispy and golden brown. Transfer the cooked fritters to a plate lined with kitchen paper to absorb the excess oil. Repeat this process with the rest of the batter.

7 Serve the *tomatokeftédes* with a sprinkle of salt and enjoy them warm.

REVYTHOKEFTÉDES

Chickpea Patties

These deliciously herby and fragrant chickpea patties are baked in the oven, unlike my recipes for *tomatokeftédes* and *kolokythokeftédes*, which are pan-fried. Golden on the outside and creamy in texture on the inside, these patties come together by whipping the ingredients to a silky-smooth consistency. I like to roughly mash some of the chickpeas and combine this with the whipped mixture to create some chunky texture in every bite. *Revythokeftédes* are delicious on their own or pair perfectly with tzatziki or tahini dip (see pages 23 and 25).

SERVES 3–4

2 × 400g (14oz) cans chickpeas, drained and rinsed

1 red onion, chopped

10g (¼oz) parsley

10g (¼oz) dill fronds

10g (¼oz) mint leaves

4 tablespoons extra virgin olive oil

juice of ½ lemon

1 teaspoon ground cumin

½ teaspoon ground coriander

½ teaspoon ground black pepper

75g (2½oz) plain flour

½ teaspoon bicarbonate of soda

salt to taste

1 Preheat the oven to 180°C fan (400°F), Gas Mark 6 and line a large baking tray with baking paper. Tip half the chickpeas into a mixing bowl and set aside. Add the other half to a food processor with the chopped onion, fresh herbs, 2 tablespoons of the oil, the lemon juice, spices and salt. Blitz for 1–2 minutes until the mixture is completely smooth.

2 Roughly mash the chickpeas in the bowl to a chunky consistency and combine the smooth whipped up chickpeas in the same bowl. Stir through the flour and bicarbonate of soda and mix until everything is incorporated.

3 Brush a tablespoon of the oil over the lined tray. Take a heaped tablespoon of the mixture, place it on the baking tray and flatten with the back of the spoon to form a patty shape. Repeat this with the rest of the mixture, leaving space between each patty.

4 Bake for 30 minutes, or until the *revythokeftédes* are golden brown on top. Let them cool for 10 minutes before serving and enjoy them with tzatziki or tahini dip. They can be stored in an airtight container in the fridge for up to 2 days.

AIR FRYER You can reheat *revythokeftédes* in an air fryer at 180°C (350°F) for 3 minutes.

KOLOKYTHOKEFTÉDES

Courgette Fritters

Every bit as popular across Greece as *tomatokeftédes* are these crispy *kolokythokeftédes*, which translates literally as courgette koftas. They're made with grated courgette, a healthy amount of fresh dill, mint and basil, and crumbled feta. The combination of these few ingredients is delightful, and these fritters make the perfect summer appetizer.

SERVES 4–6

2 courgettes, trimmed

2 spring onions, finely chopped

50g (1¾oz) dill fronds, chopped

30g (1oz) mint leaves, chopped

30g (1oz) basil leaves, chopped

250g (9oz) plain flour

2 large eggs

200g (7oz) feta cheese, crumbled

250ml (9fl oz) vegetable oil, for frying

salt and pepper

1 Start by coarsely grating the courgettes – I like to do this straight into a large bowl. Stir through the spring onions and herbs.

2 Sift over the flour then add the eggs, crumbled feta and seasoning, and gently mix to form a batter – you can do this with a spoon or by hand.

3 Pour the oil into a large frying pan and place over a high heat. Leave to heat up for about 2 minutes. Meanwhile, take a heaped tablespoonful of the batter, flatten into the palm of your hand and mould into a patty shape. Continue with the remaining batter – you should be able to make 18–20 fritters.

4 Carefully place the fritters, one by one, into the hot oil, making sure not to overcrowd the pan – it's best to cook the fritters in batches.

5 Fry the fritters for 2–3 minutes on each side, or until they become a dark golden colour. Lower the temperature if necessary to ensure that they don't burn. You will only need to flip each fritter once.

6 Transfer the cooked fritters to a plate lined with kitchen paper to absorb the excess oil. Repeat this process with the remaining fritters.

7 Serve the fritters warm.

TYROKROKÉTES ME KATAÏFI

Cheese Croquettes with Kataïfi

Kataïfi (shredded filo) is really having its moment on the internet right now. I love chopping it into short lengths to use as a crust. So let me introduce you to kataïfi-coated *tyrokrokétes*, the crispiest cheese balls. These are even more delicious than the ones I originally shared on social media. Perfect as an appetizer to serve to friends or, if you're a cheese enthusiast like me, devour all by yourself!

MAKES 10

70g (2½oz) kataïfi (shredded filo), chopped (see tip on page 46)

1 heaped teaspoon black sesame seeds

1 heaped teaspoon white sesame seeds

100g (3½oz) Cheddar cheese, grated

100g (3½oz) Gruyère cheese, grated

100g (3½oz) feta cheese, crumbled

60g (2¼oz) self-raising flour

generous 3 tablespoons full-fat milk

1 egg, beaten

200ml (7fl oz) vegetable or sunflower oil

runny honey, for drizzling (optional)

1 To prepare the kataïfi coating, put the shredded filo in a bowl with the black and white sesame seeds and mix together to combine. Set aside.

2 Add the grated Cheddar and Gruyère to another mixing bowl along with the crumbled feta, the flour, milk and egg. Mix everything together to form a sticky mixture. I do this by hand, wearing disposable gloves, but you can also mix with a spoon.

3 Take about a tablespoon of the mixture and roll it in the palm of your hands to form a ball. Roll it in the kataïfi mixture, making sure it is coated evenly on all sides. Repeat this process until you have 10 balls. (You can double-coat them if any kataïfi remains.) Line a plate with kitchen paper, ready to absorb the oil from the *tyrokrokétes* once they're fried.

4 Heat the oil in a large frying pan over a high heat. To test whether it's hot enough, stick the tip of a wooden spoon in the pan to see if the oil bubbles up around it. Carefully place the cheese balls, one at a time, in the pan, leaving space between them (cook in batches if necessary). Fry, turning regularly, for 3–4 minutes or until they become golden brown and crispy on all sides. Transfer them to the lined plate to remove any excess oil.

5 Serve your crispy cheese balls warm, either on their own or with a little honey drizzled on top.

KATAÏFI SAGANÁKI

Kataïfi-crusted Pan-fried Cheese

SERVES 3–4

20g (¾oz) plain flour

1 egg, well beaten

30g (1oz) kataïfi (shredded filo), chopped (see tip)

1 heaped teaspoon black sesame seeds

1 block Kefalotýri cheese, or substitute with 1 block Kasseri or Gruyère (about 200g/8oz)

4 teaspoons vegetable or sunflower oil

runny honey, for drizzling (optional)

TOP TIP

Kataïfi is ready-shredded filo pastry that comes in long lengths. You will need to chop it into small shreds of 2cm (¾ inch) using scissors to use it as a coating.

Saganáki is the Greek term for various dishes made with fried cheese – the name refers to the small two-handled pan traditionally used to fry the cheese. Here, I'm coating the cheese with kataïfi (shredded filo), which makes for a perfectly crispy crust. In Greece, *saganáki* is made with Kefalotýri or Kasseri – hard nutty cheeses made from either sheep or goats' milk – but you can use Gruyère or another hard cheese with a similar flavour profile. I love to top off the *saganáki* with a drizzle of honey because there's no better sweet and savoury combination.

1 Line up 4 plates to prepare the *saganáki* for frying. Add the flour to the first, the beaten egg to the second, and the kataïfi and sesame seeds (stirred to combine evenly) to the third. Place a few sheets of kitchen paper on the fourth plate, ready to absorb the excess oil from the *saganáki* once fried.

2 Run the block of cheese under cold running water and shake off any excess droplets. Immediately dredge the cheese in the flour, coating all sides well. You may need to repeat this several times to make sure the flour sticks to the cheese. Then dip it in the egg wash, coating all sides completely (again, you may wish to repeat this a few times). Finally, coat the cheese in the kataïfi mixture, covering all sides evenly. If any of the mixture remains, pat the top of the cheese with it.

3 Pour the oil into a frying pan and place over a high heat. To check it's hot enough, put a few shreds of kataïfi in the pan; if the oil bubbles up around them, it's the right temperature. Carefully place the cheese in the middle of the pan and fry on all sides for 1–2 minutes until the surface becomes golden and crispy.

4 Place the *saganáki* on the plate lined with kitchen paper and pat the sides and top to soak up the surplus oil. Slice and serve it soon after – eat it while it's still warm and gooey in the middle. If you wish, drizzle a little honey on top.

TIGANÍTA KOLOKYTHÁKIA

Crispy Courgette Chips

SERVES 4

1 courgette, trimmed and sliced very thinly (no more than 2mm/¹⁄₁₆ inch thick)

500ml (18fl oz) vegetable or sunflower oil

For the coating

80g (3oz) plain flour
80g (3oz) fine semolina
1 teaspoon dried oregano
1 teaspoon salt
½ teaspoon ground black pepper

No mezze spread is complete without *tiganíta kolokythákia* – courgette chips coated in a blend of flour and fine semolina and fried until perfectly golden. To achieve the ultimate crispy chips the key is to slice the courgette thinly, then draw out the moisture by salting, and double-coat before frying.

1 Spread out the courgette slices on a tray or clean work surface and sprinkle with half the salt. Leave for 10 minutes for the salt to draw out some of the moisture.

2 Meanwhile, set up 2 bowls. Fill one with 250ml (9fl oz) water and add to the other the flour, semolina, oregano and the remaining salt and the pepper. Stir the dry ingredients to blend and set aside. Line a plate with kitchen paper, ready to drain the fried slices.

3 Pour the oil into a saucepan 22cm (8½ inches) in diameter. Heat over a high heat for 2–4 minutes. To check the oil is hot enough, stick the tip of a wooden spoon in the pan to see if the oil bubbles up around it.

4 By this point, the courgette slices will have released some moisture, which will help the coating to stick. Coat a first batch of 6–8 slices in the dry ingredients then transfer to a plate. Quickly dip each courgette slice into the bowl of water for no longer than a second and immediately coat again in the flour mixture.

5 Carefully lower the courgette slices, one by one, into the hot oil. Do not overcrowd the pan or the oil temperature will drop, preventing the courgette slices from crisping up. For this reason I recommend frying in batches. Cook the courgette for 1–2 minutes until the slices turn golden brown. Using a wire strainer or slotted spoon, remove the slices from the oil and place them on the lined plate to remove the excess oil. Repeat this process with the remaining slices.

6 Once all the courgette slices are fried and crispy, lightly season them with salt and enjoy them warm. *Kolokythákia* can be reheated in an air fryer as with calamari (see tip on page 64).

PIPERIÉS SAGANÁKI

Pan-fried Peppers and Feta

Piperiés saganáki is a simple yet unbelievably flavour-packed appetizer made from green peppers that are charred then simmered in a fresh tomato sauce enriched with crumbled feta. I like to add dried chilli flakes for heat, but most importantly I season generously with salt and pepper to draw out the smoky flavour of the charred peppers. This is one of several *saganáki* dishes in the book and it's usually served directly from the pan while still warm. So it's perfect for placing in the middle of the table and serving to friends with any choice of bread.

SERVES 4

300g (10½oz) long green peppers (about 4), stems and seeds removed, and halved lengthways

600g (1lb 5oz) vine tomatoes

generous 4 tablespoons extra virgin olive oil

1 teaspoon caster sugar

¼ teaspoon chilli flakes (optional)

1½ teaspoons salt (or to taste)

½ teaspoon ground black pepper

100g (3½oz) feta cheese, crumbled

1 Slice the pepper halves widthways into slices 1cm (½ inch) wide and set aside.

2 Cut the tomatoes into quarters and blitz them to a pulp in a food processor. (Alternatively grate them by hand.) Scrape into a bowl and set aside.

3 Pour 3 tablespoons of the extra virgin olive oil into a large frying pan and place over a medium heat. Allow to heat up for 2 minutes before adding the green peppers. Stir them through the oil and cover the pan with a lid. Cook them for 15 minutes, stirring 2–3 times as they cook and putting the lid back on. The peppers will soften and char slightly, which is what gives the dish its distinct smoky flavour.

4 Pour in the tomatoes and stir them through the peppers. Add the sugar, dried chilli flakes, and season generously with salt and pepper. Put the lid back on and cook for another 15 minutes.

5 Remove the lid and continue cooking for a further 10–12 minutes to allow the tomatoes to reduce and the sauce to thicken. At the end of this time, and just before removing the pan from the heat, add the crumbled feta and mix well to combine. The feta will melt and homogenize with the tomato sauce.

6 Serve the *piperiés saganáki* drizzled with the remaining olive oil. Enjoy it warm with flatbread (see page 57) or pitta bread (see pages 58–60).

RAVASÁKI

Fried Feta Cheese Parcel

Owing to its parcel-like appearance, this filo-wrapped version of *saganáki* is often anecdotally referred to as *ravasáki*, which translates as 'love letter'. Gooey feta cheese wrapped in golden, perfectly crisp filo pastry would certainly be my idea of a love letter! Once fried, the *ravasáki* is topped with honey and sesame seeds. It's a beautiful salty–sweet combination and comes together in under 20 minutes, making it a wonderful dish to serve guests (or yourself!) when you don't have much time on your hands.

SERVES 2

3 filo pastry sheets

5 tablespoons extra virgin olive oil

½ block feta cheese (cut horizontally from a 200g/7oz block)

20–30g (¾–1oz) runny honey

1 teaspoon white sesame seeds

1 teaspoon black sesame seeds

1 Lay out the filo pastry sheets on a work surface and put 2 tablespoons of the oil in a bowl. Brush the surface of one sheet with oil, lay the second sheet of filo on top and brush that too, then repeat with the third sheet.

2 Place the block of feta in the middle of the filo. Fold over the bottom edge of the pastry layers first, then the top, then bring the sides to the middle, encasing the feta as if you're wrapping a parcel.

3 Pour the remaining 3 tablespoons of oil in a frying pan and place this over a medium–high heat. After a minute, add the feta parcel and fry on both sides for 1–2 minutes until golden and crispy.

4 Place the *ravasáki* on a plate lined with kitchen paper to absorb any excess oil. Next, transfer it to a serving plate and top with the honey and sesame seeds. Serve warm.

BOUGIOURNTÍ

Layered Feta and Tomato Bake

Bougiourntí is a dish I turn to time and time again because it requires very little effort to make and is the perfect heartwarming option when you just want to dive into a bowl of melted cheese. Originating from Thessaloniki, *bougiourntí* is a baked feta dip, with layers of sliced beef tomatoes, red peppers from a jar and plenty of crumbled feta paired with hard grated cheese, typically Kasseri. Since this cheese is tricky to find outside of Greece, I opt for grated mozzarella to create that characteristic stringy cheese pull that we all know and love.

SERVES 2–3

1 large beef tomato or 2 medium ones, thinly sliced

200g (7oz) feta cheese, crumbled

30g (1oz) Kasseri, hard mozzarella or Gruyère cheese, grated

2 tablespoons roasted red peppers from a jar, chopped

1–2 pickled green chillies, chopped

½ teaspoon dried oregano

drizzle of extra virgin olive oil

1 Preheat the oven to 200°C fan (425°F), Gas Mark 7. Form a layer of sliced tomatoes in a tapas or Camembert baking dish. Top them with the crumbled feta, then your choice of grated cheese.

2 Spread the chopped peppers and chillies evenly over the cheese. Season with the oregano and a drizzle of olive oil.

3 Cover the dish with a lid or foil and bake for 15 minutes, then uncover and bake for a further 5 minutes until the top is golden and crispy.

4 Serve the *bougiourntí* warm with flatbread (see page 57) or pitta bread (see pages 58–60).

DOLMADÁKIA

Stuffed Vine Leaves

MAKES ABOUT 30

260–300g (9½–10½oz) vine leaves in brine, stalks removed

1 lemon, sliced thinly

100ml (3½fl oz) extra virgin olive oil, plus a little for brushing

500ml (18fl oz) hot water

For the filling

100ml (3½fl oz) extra virgin olive oil

2 echalion shallots, finely chopped

10 spring onions, finely chopped

2 garlic cloves, grated or crushed

250g (9oz) long-grain rice

juice of 1 lemon

½ teaspoon ground black pepper

50g (1¾oz) mint leaves, finely chopped

50g (1¾oz) fresh coriander, finely chopped

50g (1¾oz) dill fronds, finely chopped

salt to taste

Nothing reminds me more of Greece than stuffed vine leaves, or *dolmadákia*. Enjoyed in many countries and in many ways, the Greek version of this iconic dish uses plenty of fresh herbs, extra virgin olive oil and lemon juice, simmered until the rice is perfectly tender. They're surprisingly easy to whip up; you just need to be patient when it comes to rolling the stuffed vine leaves. It's worth making these in advance because the flavours settle and become even more lemony and delicious as the *dolmadákia* cool down.

1 First prepare the filling. Pour the oil into a large, lidded frying pan over a medium heat. Add the shallots, spring onions and garlic. Stir to combine, cover the pan with a lid and leave the onions to cook for 10 minutes, stirring halfway through. By this point, the onions will be soft and translucent.

2 Wash the rice, rinsing until the water runs clear. Drain, then add to the frying pan, along with 250ml (9fl oz) of hot water, the lemon juice, pepper and salt to taste. Cover the pan again and leave to cook for 6–7 minutes until the liquid reduces and the rice is al dente (it will cook fully when wrapped in the leaves). Add the chopped herbs to the rice and stir to combine well. Remove from the heat and set aside to cool a little.

3 Meanwhile, rinse the vine leaves under cold water to remove the flavour of the brine. Brush the bottom of a deep saucepan with a little olive oil, line it with 6–8 overlapping vine leaves then top with the lemon slices.

4 To make the *dolmadákia*, open out a vine leaf on a work surface or board, veined side face up and shiny side face down. Place a heaped tablespoon of the rice mixture in the centre, and fold in the bottom of the leaf over the rice and then fold in the sides. Roll to form a small log shape and transfer this to the saucepan with the seam-side underneath. Repeat the process with the rest of the filling, using as many vine leaves as you need – you should be able to make 30 rolls. Place the stuffed vine leaves one next to the other. When the first layer is complete, place the rest on top to create another one or two layers.

5 Pour the oil and the remaining 250ml (9fl oz) of hot water on top and cover the stuffed vine leaves with a plate. This weighs them down and allows them to soften and become tender without falling apart. Cover the saucepan with a lid and place over a medium heat. Cook for a total of 1 hour, removing the lid halfway through, and removing the plate 10 minutes before the end of the cooking time. Once there is no liquid remaining, remove the pan from the heat. Ideally, leave the *dolmadákia* to cool for at least an hour; this ensures they stay intact and they taste even better cold, although they can also be enjoyed warm.

PÍTES

Greek Flatbreads

I proudly call this recipe the best for homemade Greek flatbreads, with hundreds of thousands of people saving it on social media. They're super easy to make and come together with just a handful of store-cupboard ingredients. I prefer to use honey instead of sugar for the dough as it makes the flatbreads really soft. They're a must-have when serving chicken gyros (see my recipe on page 133) and taste way better than shop-bought versions. Plus, they keep well in either the fridge or freezer – just reheat them in the toaster before serving!

MAKES 8

300ml (10fl oz) lukewarm water

7g (1 sachet) fast-action dried yeast

1 teaspoon runny honey

500g (1lb 2oz) strong white bread flour, plus extra for dusting

pinch of salt

olive oil, for frying

1. Pour the lukewarm water into a large mixing bowl. Add the yeast and honey to the bowl and whisk until the mixture is frothy. Leave this to settle for 2 minutes.

2. Sift in the flour and mix into the liquid using a wooden spoon to form a dough. Transfer the dough to a stand mixer fitted with a dough hook and knead for 2–3 minutes or tip on to a clean work surface and knead by hand for 5 minutes. Add a pinch of salt halfway through and continue kneading to incorporate.

3. Once the dough is firm, pinch and tuck in the sides to form a dough ball and lightly dust with flour. Place it back in the large mixing bowl and cover it with a clean tea towel. Leave at room temperature to prove for 30 minutes until risen and doubled in size.

4. Divide the proved dough into 8 equal pieces and roll to form smaller dough balls. Leave them to prove again for a further 10 minutes.

5. Lightly dust your work surface and, one at a time, flatten the dough balls using a rolling pin. The flatbreads should be round and roughly 2mm (1/16 inch) thick. Then create dimples on the flatbreads by pressing your fingertips over the top.

6. Add a drizzle of olive oil to a frying pan and place over a medium heat. After a minute, add one flatbread at a time and fry for 1–2 minutes on each side. Repeat to cook the rest of the flatbreads, adding a drizzle of oil to the pan each time.

7. The flatbreads are best served warm. Enjoy with gyros or with dips.

KYPRIAKÉS PÍTES

Cypriot Pitta Bread

There's something so special about homemade pitta bread and it genuinely doesn't get better than this recipe, which reminds me of the pitta bread I grew up eating with souvlaki. The dough is made using Greek yogurt, which gives the pittas a uniquely soft and spongy texture with a crispy crust. They're perfect for devouring on their own, especially when still warm; for stuffing with grilled meats or veg; or simply slicing for scooping up your favourite dips (the classics being hummus and tzatziki).

MAKES 10

300ml (10fl oz) lukewarm water

1 tablespoon caster sugar

7g (1 sachet) fast-action dried yeast

650g (1lb 7oz) strong white bread flour, plus extra for dusting

150g (5½oz) Greek yogurt (10% fat)

2 tablespoons extra virgin olive oil

½ teaspoon salt

1. Pour the lukewarm water into a large mixing bowl or use a stand mixer. Whisk in the sugar by hand then add the yeast and whisk again to dissolve. Leave the yeast to settle for 2 minutes before sifting in the flour and adding the yogurt. If using a stand mixer, attach the dough hook and knead the dough on a low speed for 6 minutes. If kneading by hand, mix the ingredients with a wooden spoon to homogenize the dough in the bowl before turning it out on to a lightly floured work surface and knead for about 12 minutes or until firm but malleable.

2. Add the olive oil and salt and knead for a further 6 minutes to incorporate until the dough becomes smooth. Pinch and tuck in the bottom of the dough to form a ball, lightly dust the top with flour then place the dough ball back in the bowl. Cover with a clean tea towel and leave at room temperature to prove for an hour until risen and doubled in size.

3. Once the dough has risen, remove it from the bowl and weigh it: it should be about 1.15kg (2lb 8oz). Divide it into 10 equal pieces, roughly 115g (4oz), and roll them into balls on a lightly floured surface. Cover and leave them to prove again for another 15 minutes. At this point, preheat the oven to your oven's highest setting and line a large baking tray with baking paper.

4 Once the oven has reached temperature, begin rolling out the balls into long thin oval shapes (this is the classic Cypriot pitta bread shape), roughly 20cm (8 inches) long and 8–10cm (3–4 inches) wide. You may need to flour the surface before rolling out each ball to make sure they don't stick.

5 Lay 2 pittas on the lined baking tray, spaced apart, and place the tray on the middle rack. Cook for a total of 6 minutes but set a timer for 4 or 5 minutes, because they will puff up at this point and will need to be quickly flipped over and cooked for 1–2 minutes on the other side.

6 Transfer the cooked pittas to a plate and wrap with a clean tea towel to keep them warm. Cook the rest, 2 at a time, for 6 minutes in total as before.

7 The pittas remain soft even after several hours of baking them. You can reheat them in the toaster or store them, wrapped in foil, in the fridge where they will keep for up to 2 days.

KYPRIAKÓ CHORIÁTIKO PSOMI

Cypriot Village Bread

SERVES 4–6

175ml (6fl oz) lukewarm full-fat milk

125ml (4fl oz) lukewarm water

1 teaspoon caster sugar

7g (1 sachet) fast-action dried yeast

500g (1lb 2oz) strong white bread flour, plus extra for dusting

1 teaspoon ground mahlepi

1 teaspoon ground mastic

8 teaspoons extra virgin olive oil, plus extra for brushing

1 teaspoon salt

For the coating

1 teaspoon cumin seeds

2 teaspoons aniseed

2 teaspoons white sesame seeds

2 teaspoons black sesame seeds

2 teaspoons full-fat milk

This gorgeously fragrant tear-and-share Cypriot village bread should be the centrepiece of any mezze spread. Covered in sesame seeds and whole spices, the contrast of a crunchy, aromatic crust with a light and bouncy crumb is what makes this bread truly one of a kind. The dough contains full-fat milk, which gives the bread its soft texture, along with mahlepi (made from ground cherry kernels) and mastic (a type of resin), which provide a distinctive aroma. It's not only delicious but also visually impressive – guaranteed to be the star of the show at any gathering.

1 Select 2 large mixing bowls. In one of them, combine the lukewarm milk and water, the sugar and yeast and whisk together. Leave the yeast to settle for 2 minutes. Meanwhile, place the flour, mahlepi and mastic in the second bowl and stir to together. Pour the oil into the flour bowl and rub it into the flour with your hands to form a crumbly mixture – this helps to give the bread its distinctive texture.

2 Make a well in the centre of the flour and slowly pour in the yeast mixture. Stir using your hands or a wooden spoon to form a dough.

3 Transfer the dough either to a stand mixer fitted with the dough hook or on to a lightly floured work surface. Knead the dough for 10 minutes if using a stand mixer or 20 minutes if kneading by hand, adding the salt halfway through.

4 Roll the kneaded dough into a ball and lightly brush the top with olive oil – just enough to give it some shine. Put the dough ball back into the mixing bowl, cover it with a clean tea towel and leave at room temperature to prove for 2 hours or until risen and doubled in size.

5 Meanwhile, line a large baking tray with baking paper. Mix the cumin, aniseed and sesame seeds together in a small bowl then spread them over the lined tray, ready to coat the dough.

»

6 After 2 hours, transfer the risen dough on to a lightly floured surface. Gently stretch and roll it to form a sausage shape, sealing the edges as you lengthen it. The dough should be about 30–35cm (12–14 inches) long.

7 Brush the milk all over the dough and transfer to the baking tray. Carefully roll it in the seed mixture to cover it on all sides. Use a sharp knife to score the dough 7 or 8 times without cutting right through. Then cover the dough with the tea towel and leave to prove again for 30 minutes.

8 Meanwhile, preheat the oven to 220°C fan (475°F), Gas Mark 9. Pour 150ml (5fl oz) of water into an ovenproof dish, ready to place in the bottom of the oven at the same time the bread is baking. (This will create steam in the oven and will give the bread a lighter and airy texture.)

9 Once the bread has proved for a second time, remove the tea towel and slide the tray on to the middle shelf of the hot oven, with the dish of water under it. Bake for a total of 28–30 minutes, reducing the temperature to 180°C fan (400°F), Gas Mark 6 after 15 minutes, until the bread is golden brown and aromatic. Remove and leave the bread to rest for 15–20 minutes before tucking in.

TOP TIP If you cannot find mahlepi and mastic, ground cardamom and ground aniseed are suitable alternative spice flavours.

KALAMÁRI

Calamari

SERVES 4

450g (1lb) prepared calamari tubes, sliced into rings 1–2cm (½–¾ inch) wide
750ml (1⅓ pints) vegetable or sunflower oil, for frying
½ lemon, for squeezing

For the coating
100g (3½oz) plain flour
30g (1oz) fine semolina
30g (1oz) cornflour
pinch of ground turmeric
salt and pepper

AIR FRYER

Any leftover calamari rings can be reheated in an air fryer – and they will be crispy on the outside! Simply line them up in the basket, leaving space between them, and air-fry at 180°C (350°F) for 3 minutes.

Super-crispy calamari rings are quintessentially Greek – you'll find them served in most tavernas and beach restaurants in Greece. They only need about a minute in hot oil to become perfectly crispy and lightly golden on the outside, while still being soft and tender. The trick is to quickly dip the coated calamari rings in water – this makes them really crunchy. Make these and you will feel like you're on a beach on a Greek island.

1 First set up two bowls. Fill one with 200ml (7fl oz) water and add to the other the flour, semolina, cornflour, turmeric and seasoning. The ground turmeric will give the calamari rings a nice golden colour. Stir the dry ingredients well to blend and set aside. Line a plate with kitchen paper, ready to drain the fried rings.

2 Place about 5 or 6 calamari rings in the flour mixture, coating them well on both sides. I like to prepare this number of rings at a time, which gives me a batch ready to fry.

3 Pour the oil into a saucepan (I use one 22cm/8½ inches in diameter). Place over the highest heat setting and leave it for 2–4 minutes to heat. To check the oil is hot enough, stick the tip of a wooden spoon in the pan to see if the oil bubbles up around it.

4 Once the oil is hot, quickly dip the coated calamari rings, one by one, in the bowl of water for no longer than a second then dip into the batter again. Immediately and carefully lower them, one at a time, into the oil to fry for 1½ minutes – any longer and you risk overcooking them, making them chewy. Use a wire strainer or slotted spoon to remove the calamari from the oil and place them on the lined plate to remove the excess oil. Repeat this process, 5 or 6 at a time, with the remaining calamari rings.

5 Once they are all fried, lightly season the crispy rings with salt, add a squeeze of lemon juice and enjoy them warm.

KEFTEDÁKIA

Greek Meatballs

These are not your average meatballs. They are irresistibly crispy on the outside, juicy on the inside, herby and packed with flavour! *Keftédes*, or *keftedákia* which, in this context, just means baby meatballs, are a staple appetizer in Greece. Grating, not chopping, the red onion, plus the combination of minced beef and pork makes the *keftédes* naturally tender and moist as well as rich in flavour. And trust me when I say that the more generous you are with the fresh mint, the tastier the result: the mint cuts through the fattiness of the meat and makes the *keftedákia* beautifully aromatic, so I recommend using a solid handful of leaves. I love serving these warm with my homemade tzatziki (see page 23).

SERVES 4

1 red onion, grated

2 garlic cloves, grated

20g (¾oz) mint leaves, finely chopped

1 large egg

100g (3½oz) homemade breadcrumbs (toasted then blitzed)

2 tablespoons extra virgin olive oil

500g (1lb 2oz) minced pork (10% fat)

250g (9oz) minced beef (5% fat)

100g (3½oz) plain flour, for dredging

1 litre (1¾ pints) vegetable or sunflower oil, for frying

salt and pepper

1 Place the grated onion and garlic in a large mixing bowl. Add the mint, egg, breadcrumbs, oil, minced meats and seasoning and give everything a good mix to combine the ingredients. (I like to do this by hand using disposable gloves as this allows me to distribute the ingredients with more control than with a spoon.)

2 Grab 2 plates and sieve the flour on one of them. Take a heaped tablespoon of the mixture and roll to form a meatball. Place on the second plate. Repeat to make about 16 meatballs with the rest of the mixture. Dredge each meatball in the flour, making sure you cover them evenly.

3 Pour the oil into a large, deep-sided saucepan and place over a high heat. Once the oil is hot enough (you can test this by sticking the tip of a wooden spoon in the pan and seeing if the oil bubbles up around it), carefully lower in the meatballs one by one. I recommend cooking them in batches to avoid overcrowding the pan and to ensure that the meatballs cook evenly. Fry the *keftedákia* for 7–8 minutes, turning them occasionally, until they become golden brown on all sides. Repeat this process with the remaining meatballs (cook in 2–3 batches, depending on the size of the pan). As the oil becomes hotter you may find the succeeding batches cook more quickly.

4 Transfer the cooked batches to a plate lined with kitchen paper to absorb the excess oil. Enjoy them warm.

lads Like a

3. Salac

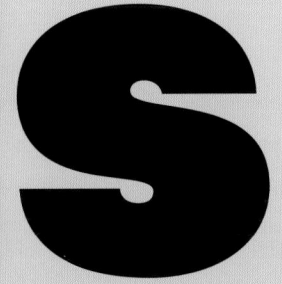

Let me introduce you to ten of the best Greek salads – some you'll have heard of and others should go on your to-try list. How about **maroulosaláta** – a fresh, crunchy and herby lettuce salad that goes with everything – or **pantzarosaláta**, a creamy, nutty, tangy beetroot salad that's the perfect accompaniment to roasted or grilled meats? There's the iconic **horiátiki saláta**, universally known – and enjoyed – as Greek village salad. You'll also find salads that will up your barbecue and picnic game, like the gorgeously garlicky Cypriot potato salad called **Kypriakí patatosaláta**, or **láchanosaláta** – a crunchy cabbage salad with a vibrant dressing. But when you're not in the mood to chop and still want something refreshingly good, a simple **watermelon and feta salad** is unbeatable on a hot summer's day.

KYPRIAKÍ PATATOSALÁTA

Cypriot-style Potato Salad

It's such a treat when thin-skinned Cyprus potatoes appear in the shops. The island's rich volcanic soils give them a distinctly nutty taste, which is showcased in this salad, enriched with garlic, lemon juice, olive oil and fresh parsley. This is a staple in my household whenever we light our barbecue, because it's simple to prepare, bursts with flavour and pairs perfectly with grilled meats.

SERVES 4

1kg (2lb 4oz) unpeeled baby potatoes, preferably Cyprus, rinsed

3 garlic cloves, crushed

juice of 2 lemons

100ml (3½fl oz) extra virgin olive oil

50g (1¾oz) parsley, finely chopped

salt to taste

1 Put the potatoes in a large saucepan and cover fully with water. Place over a medium heat and boil for 25 minutes, or until the potatoes have softened. Drain then fill the pan with cold water and allow the potatoes to cool for a minute, then drain again.

2 Cut the cooled potatoes in half, depending on size, and transfer to a large serving bowl. Add the garlic, lemon juice, olive oil and parsley. Season with salt to taste. Mix everything together until the potatoes are evenly coated and serve.

SALÁTA MELITZÁNAS PSITÍ

Roasted Aubergine Salad

I've not stopped thinking about this salad ever since I first tried it on holiday in Corfu. The tender, slow-cooked aubergine and slightly charred sweet red peppers dressed in a garlicky olive oil concoction, had me hooked for years. It's no wonder I found myself at the same taverna several times in one week. I've not been able to find it again, so I've recreated it in the way that I recall with a few additions: walnuts for crunch and spring onions for freshness. It's an absolute flavour bomb.

SERVES 2

1 aubergine, trimmed, halved lengthways and thinly sliced into crescents (about 5mm/¼ inch thick)

1 tablespoon extra virgin olive oil

1 pointed red pepper, halved, stem and seeds removed

60g (2¼oz) rocket leaves

50g (1¾oz) walnuts, roughly chopped

2 spring onions, finely chopped

For the dressing

3 tablespoons extra virgin olive oil

1½ tablespoons white wine vinegar

1 garlic clove, crushed

salt to taste

1 Preheat the oven to 180°C fan (400°F), Gas Mark 6. Place the aubergine slices on a baking tray lined with baking paper and lightly brush the oil on top. Bake for 40 minutes, turning them over after 20 minutes. At this point, add the halved red pepper to the tray to cook for the remaining 20 minutes.

2 Place the veg in a bowl and cover with clingfilm. Leave for 30 minutes – trapping in the moisture will make them even more tender and soft. Peel off the pepper's thin skin and thinly slice the halves.

3 Assemble the salad by adding the rocket leaves, walnuts, spring onions and veg to a large bowl. Put the ingredients for the dressing in a cup or jar and stir gently to combine. Pour over the salad and toss everything to mix well before serving.

ELLINIKÍ KRITHAROSALÁTA

Greek-style Orzo Salad

Orzo is used to make this super-easy Greek-style pasta salad, tossed in a banging dressing made using Dijon mustard. So much of Greek cuisine includes the glorious herbs that flourish in the country's rocky terrain and here, plenty of dill and mint bring extra fresh flavour – it's the perfect summer salad.

SERVES 4

- 300g (10½oz) orzo
- 4 baby or Lebanese cucumbers, chopped into small chunks
- 12–14 cherry tomatoes, quartered
- 1 small red onion, finely chopped
- handful of dill fronds, finely chopped
- handful of mint leaves, finely chopped
- 200g (7oz) feta cheese, crumbled

For the dressing

- 4–5 tablespoons extra virgin olive oil (adjusting to taste)
- 3 tablespoons red wine vinegar, adding more to taste
- 2 teaspoons Dijon mustard
- salt and pepper

1 Cook the orzo in a saucepan of boiling water over a medium heat following the packet instructions (this normally takes 9–11 minutes).

2 Meanwhile, prepare the salad ingredients and transfer everything to a large serving bowl. When the orzo is cooked, drain through a sieve and run it under cold water to cool. Once fully drained and cooled, add the orzo to the bowl.

3 Mix the ingredients for the dressing in a cup or jar and pour over the salad. Crumble the feta on top and mix to coat everything before serving.

LÁCHANOSALÁTA

Cabbage Slaw

This addictive crunchy, herby cabbage salad is simple to whip up and is a versatile side dish that can be paired with all sorts of fish and grilled meats. Thinly sliced red and white cabbage, grated carrots and finely chopped spring onions and dill are all brought together with a tangy dressing that keeps the salad bright and fresh even a day after!

SERVES 6–8

½ purple cabbage with thick outer leaves removed, halved

½ white cabbage with thick outer leaves removed, halved

2 carrots, grated

2 spring onions, finely chopped

50–60g (1¾–2¼oz) dill fronds, finely chopped

For the dressing

2 teaspoons Dijon mustard

100ml (3½fl oz) extra virgin olive oil

4–5 tablespoons white wine vinegar

salt and pepper

1 Taking a quarter at a time, slice the purple and white cabbages on a mandolin to achieve thin shavings. Alternatively, if you don't have a mandolin, simply cut the cabbages into very thin strips. Put the strips in a large salad bowl, along with the grated carrots, chopped spring onions and dill fronds.

2 Put the ingredients for the dressing in a cup or jar and stir gently to combine. Pour this over the salad and toss to mix everything together well.

3 Serve immediately or store the *láchanosaláta* in an airtight container in the fridge and eat within 2 days.

ELLINIKÍ HORIÁTIKI SALÁTA

Greek Village Salad

I just had to include the iconic *horiátiki saláta*, widely known as traditional Greek village salad. What really elevates *horiátiki saláta* is the gorgeous red wine vinegar dressing: be sure to soak up every last drop with crusty bread!

SERVES 4

1 cucumber

450g (1lb) vine tomatoes, quartered

1 red onion, thinly sliced

1 green pepper, stem and seeds removed, thinly sliced

100g (3½oz) pitted Kalamata olives

200g (7oz) feta cheese, broken into chunks

For the dressing

2–3 teaspoons dried mint

4 tablespoons extra virgin olive oil

3 tablespoons red wine vinegar

salt to taste

1 Peel the cucumber and slice it in half, lengthways. Use a spoon to scoop out all the seeds then cut it into 1–2mm (1/16 inch) slices. Transfer to a large salad bowl along with the tomatoes, the onion and pepper slices, and pitted olives.

2 Put the ingredients for the dressing in a cup or jar and stir gently to combine. Pour this over the salad.

3 Add the feta chunks, mix the salad to coat everything in the dressing and serve.

ELLINIKÍ PANTZANÉLA

Greek-style Panzanella

Panzanella originated in Italy as a way of using up stale bread. This Greek take on the salad, using thinly sliced red onion, crumbled feta and ciabatta croutons baked with fresh oregano until perfectly crunchy, is not only delightful to eat but also looks impressive. You can't beat its simple flavour combination, elevated with a garnish of oregano and basil for freshness. Make sure you toss the salad in the dressing before adding the croutons so that they maintain their crunch.

SERVES 4

150g (5½oz) ciabatta, broken into bite-sized chunks

10 oregano leaves, finely chopped

4 teaspoons extra virgin olive oil

2 vine tomatoes, roughly chopped

150g (5½oz) cherry tomatoes, halved

½ red onion, thinly sliced

120g (4oz) feta cheese, crumbled

fresh oregano and basil leaves, to garnish

salt to taste

For the dressing

8 teaspoons extra virgin olive oil

4 teaspoons red wine vinegar

1 Preheat the oven to 200°C fan (425°F), Gas Mark 7. Scatter the ciabatta chunks over a large baking tray and season with the chopped oregano, extra virgin olive oil and a generous sprinkle of salt. Bake in the hot oven for 15 minutes, turning the tray halfway through, or until the ciabatta chunks are golden brown and crunchy. Set aside to cool.

2 Meanwhile prepare the vine and cherry tomatoes and add them to a mixing bowl, along with the red onion slices and feta.

3 Put the ingredients for the dressing in a cup or jar and stir gently to combine. Pour the dressing into the bowl and toss the salad ingredients to combine. Add the ciabatta chunks and gently mix again. (Adding them after the dressing means you don't get soggy croutons.)

4 Transfer the panzanella to a large serving platter and garnish with a few oregano and basil leaves, and a sprinkle of salt to taste.

MAROULOSALÁTA

Greek Lettuce Salad

This crunchy, fresh and herby Greek salad is a mix of chopped lettuce, spring onions, dill and mint, dressed in a simple yet unbeatable dressing of olive oil, lemon juice and dried oregano. I love to add crumbled feta and serve the salad with my homemade *biftékia* (see page 114) and tzatziki (see page 23) for a balanced and refreshing plate.

SERVES 4

1 Cos lettuce, finely chopped

2 spring onions, finely chopped

15g (½oz) dill fronds, finely chopped

15g (½oz) mint leaves, finely chopped

150g (5½oz) feta cheese, crumbled

For the dressing

4 tablespoons extra virgin olive oil

juice of 1 lemon

1 teaspoon dried oregano

salt to taste

1 Place the finely chopped lettuce to a large mixing bowl, followed by the spring onions and finely chopped herbs. Crumble the feta on top.

2 Prepare the dressing by mixing the oil, lemon, dried oregano and seasoning in a cup or jar and pour over the salad. Toss well to combine. Enjoy your *maroulosaláta* with grilled meat or fish, or simply on its own.

TOP TIP When using fresh dill, I separate the soft fronds from the stalks and finely chop the stalks first then the fronds.

PANTZAROSALÁTA

Beetroot Salad

Pantzarosaláta is a favourite salad in many Greek kitchens, especially when paired with souvlaki (see page 116), and, if you're not already a fan, this version will convert you! The tangy and creamy yogurt complements the earthy taste of beetroot, and walnuts add flavour and texture. Instead of roasting or boiling them from raw, I like to use ready-to-eat baby beetroots, as they're sweeter and crunchier. This salad is so easy to bring together and can be made in advance.

SERVES 4

500g (1lb 2oz) ready-to-eat baby beetroot in mild vinegar, drained and cut into 2.5cm (1 inch) cubes

1 tablespoon balsamic vinegar glaze (only use if the beetroot is not packed in vinegar)

150g (5½oz) Greek yogurt (10% fat)

generous 3 tablespoons extra virgin olive oil

3 garlic cloves, crushed

100g (3½oz) feta cheese, crumbled

50g (1¾oz) walnuts, finely chopped

salt to taste

1 Put the cubed beetroot into a mixing bowl. Add the balsamic vinegar (if using), yogurt, olive oil, garlic, feta, walnuts and salt to taste.

2 Mix everything well and serve. *Pantzarosaláta* also keeps in the fridge in an airtight container for up to 2 days.

REVYTHOSALÁTA

Chickpea Salad

Chickpeas and feta go so well together and this vibrant salad is everything I want on a plate. The cucumbers and tomatoes add crunch, the basil and mint brightness, and the olives a salty kick. I like to use jarred colossal green olives in brine as they're slightly sharper than ones marinated in oil, but if you can't find any, then I'd recommend jarred Kalamata olives – removing the pits first! *Revythosaláta* is the perfect salad when you need to get ahead or to serve at picnics, as it can be prepped in advance and stores well refrigerated.

SERVES 4

2 baby or Lebanese cucumbers (about 240g/8½oz), quartered lengthways then diced

200g (7oz) cherry tomatoes, quartered

100g (3½oz) colossal green olives, pitted and sliced

2 spring onions, finely chopped

10g (¼oz) mint leaves, finely chopped

10g (¼oz) basil leaves, finely chopped

2 × 400g (14oz) cans chickpeas, drained and rinsed

150g (5½oz) feta cheese, crumbled

For the dressing

4 tablespoons extra virgin olive oil

2 tablespoons red wine vinegar

salt and pepper

1 Put all the prepped salad ingredients in a large bowl. Add the drained chickpeas and the feta.

2 Put the ingredients for the dressing in a cup or jar and stir gently to combine. Pour over the salad and toss everything to mix well before serving. Alternatively, if you're getting ahead and keeping the salad in the fridge, don't add the dressing until just before serving, otherwise the fresh herbs will wilt.

KARPOÚZI ME FETA

Watermelon with Feta

On a hot summer's day, no salad compares to the humble *karpoúzi me feta*. Watermelons are grown in Greece, where this is a popular combination – the salty feta perfectly complementing the refreshing sweetness of watermelon. With a bit of fresh mint and a simple dressing, it's truly a chef's kiss.

SERVES 4–6

750g (1lb 10oz) watermelon flesh (about a quarter of a large watermelon), cut into chunks

100g (3½oz) feta cheese, crumbled

15g (½oz) mint leaves, finely chopped

For the dressing

20g (¾oz) runny honey

2 teaspoons balsamic vinegar

2 teaspoons extra virgin olive oil

1 Put the watermelon chunks in a large serving bowl (remove any seeds if you prefer). Add the feta and mint and mix gently.

2 Put the ingredients for the dressing in a cup or jar and stir gently to combine. Instead of pouring this into the bowl, I recommend plating up the salad first and drizzling a little dressing on each serving. This prevents the watermelon from becoming soggy.

ay

ers

Greek

4. Everyday Dinners

This is where to turn when you're craving the comfort of homecooked food but have little time on your hands. Most recipes in this chapter come together within 30 minutes – perfect for weeknights. You'll find hearty classics such as **revythía**, a chickpea soup that feels like a hug in a bowl; meat-free dishes known as **fakes**, done both the Greek and Cypriot way; and **fasoláda**, a simple yet unbelievably delicious cannellini bean staple. There are also one-pot bangers that just hit the spot: **kritharáki** – a creamy, tomatoey orzo; **spanakórizo** – a silky spinach and feta rice; and **pligoúri** – a naturally plant-based tomatoey bulgur wheat. Beyond grains and legumes, this chapter also celebrates the simplicity of Greek stews that use tomatoes and potatoes as the base: look for **fasolákia giachní**, a vegan green bean and potato stew cooked in a gorgeous tomatoey sauce, and **bámies laderés**, the name for a super-easy and rich okra stew. For meat-lovers, I've also included my **biftékia** recipe – Greek-style beef patties that people go wild for every time I share them on social media. You'll know exactly why, once you try them!

STRAPATSÁDA

Tomatoey Scrambled Eggs with Feta

Say hello to your new favourite way to eat scrambled eggs! Known to Greeks as *strapatsáda*, this dish contains a base of caramelized red onions cooked in a rich tomato sauce. Once the sauce has reduced, eggs are added to the mixture and scrambled before being topped with lots of crumbled feta for a deliciously creamy, perfectly salty finish. This dish is so quick and simple to whip up and makes for an excellent midweek dinner or weekend breakfast.

SERVES 3–4

2 tablespoons extra virgin olive oil

1 red onion, finely chopped

2 garlic cloves, grated

1 teaspoon dried oregano

1 teaspoon dried thyme

500g (1lb 2oz) vine tomatoes, grated or blitzed

2 tablespoons balsamic vinegar glaze

5 large eggs

150g (5½oz) feta cheese, crumbled, plus extra to garnish

toasted bread slices, to serve

salt and pepper

finely chopped parsley, to garnish

1 Pour the oil into a frying pan and place over a medium–high heat. After a minute, add the onion, garlic and herbs, and stir through. Cook for 2 minutes until softened.

2 Add the tomatoes along with the balsamic vinegar glaze and stir through the sautéed onion–garlic mixture. Season to taste and cook for a further 3 minutes until the sauce is reduced and the tomatoes have darkened in colour.

3 Crack in the eggs, one by and one, and use a spatula to quickly stir them through the hot tomato mixture until they have scrambled – this will take about a minute.

4 Remove the pan from the heat and crumble in the feta.

5 Serve the *strapatsáda* immediately on toast garnished with extra crumbled feta and some finely chopped parsley.

GÍGANTES PLÁKI

Greek Baked Beans

SERVES 4

3 tablespoons extra virgin olive oil

1 red onion, chopped

3 celery sticks, chopped

3 carrots, chopped

2 pointed red peppers, stems and seeds removed, chopped

3 garlic cloves, chopped

75g (2½oz) tomato purée

5 tablespoons white wine

400g (14oz) can chopped tomatoes

2 vegetable stock cubes, dissolved in 500ml (18fl oz) hot water

zest of ½ lemon

1 teaspoon ground cinnamon

2 bay leaves

3 × 400g (14oz) cans butter beans, drained and rinsed

15g (½oz) parsley, chopped

200g (7oz) feta cheese, crumbled

salt and pepper

The dish known as *gígantes pláki* epitomizes traditional Greek food and occupies a place in the hearts of most Greek households. The name comes from the 'giant' beans – often butter beans or a variety of extra-large white runner beans called *fasólia gígantes* – that are baked in a gorgeous chunky tomato stew. For ease, I'm using canned butter beans here, so that all that needs to be made is the hearty sauce to accompany them. I love to top my *gígantes pláki* with crumbled feta and bake until the cheese is beautifully golden and crispy.

1 Pour the olive oil into a large saucepan and place over a medium–high heat. After a minute, add the onion and sauté for 3 minutes until softened. Add the celery, carrots, peppers, garlic and tomato purée and sauté for a further 5 minutes, stirring regularly throughout.

2 Once the veg have softened, deglaze the pan by adding the wine, tomatoes and prepared vegetable stock. Mix until well combined.

3 Add the lemon zest, cinnamon and bay leaves and season with salt and pepper. Stir to combine then lower the heat and leave the sauce to reduce for 10 minutes.

4 Meanwhile, preheat the oven to 200°C fan (425°F), Gas Mark 7.

5 Put the butter beans in a deep baking dish (about 25 × 32cm/10 × 12½in), pour over the cooked sauce and add the parsley. Mix everything to combine then crumble the feta over, making sure most of the surface is covered. Bake for 12–15 minutes until the feta is melted and golden on top.

6 Serve warm. This is great with a side of crusty bread and Kalamata olives. Any leftovers can be refrigerated in an airtight container and enjoyed the next day.

ELLINIKÉS FAKES

Greek Lentil Soup

Fakes done the Greek way is a hearty lentil soup made with a handful of ingredients for the base, which I like to call the holy trinity of veg. Chopped onion, carrots and celery are sautéed with cumin and crushed garlic before being cooked in a broth of chopped tomatoes and vegetable stock. Just before serving, a little white wine vinegar is stirred through (this brightens the flavours of the soup). I love to serve this with Kalamata olives and crusty bread, but many Greeks enjoy the soup with a side of anchovies.

SERVES 4

3 tablespoons extra virgin olive oil
1 red onion, finely chopped
2 carrots, chopped
2 celery sticks, chopped
3 garlic cloves, grated or crushed
1 teaspoon ground cumin
1 tablespoon tomato purée
400g (14oz) can chopped tomatoes
200g (7oz) dried green lentils, rinsed and drained
1 vegetable stock cube, dissolved in 1.2 litres (2 pints) hot water
2 bay leaves
3 tablespoons white wine vinegar
salt and pepper

To serve
crusty bread
Kalamata olives

1 Pour the oil into a large saucepan placed over a medium–high heat. After a minute add the onion and cook for 2 minutes, stirring continuously, then add the carrots, celery, garlic and cumin. Cook for a further 3 minutes to soften all the vegetables.

2 Add the tomato purée, chopped tomatoes, lentils, prepared vegetable stock and bay leaves. Give everything a good mix then cover the pan with a lid and cook for 30 minutes, stirring regularly. The lentils will soften and the consistency will thicken.

3 Just before serving, season the soup generously with salt and pepper. (This is done right at the end because adding salt sooner makes the uncooked lentils harden.) Stir through the white wine vinegar.

4 Serve the soup with some crusty bread and Kalamata olives on the side.

KYPRIAKÉS FAKES

Cypriot-style Lentil Rice

I have fond memories of these Cypriot-style *fakes*, a dish my *yiayiá* (grandma) would make for us – usually on a Monday. It was typical in our household to follow the Greek Orthodox Lenten tradition of *Kathara Deftera* (Clean Monday), which marks the start of a fasting period characterized by the avoidance of meats. We'd do this regularly, not just in the days before Easter, but it never felt like we were missing out on meat because my *yiayiá*'s *fakes* were so delicious. Although she didn't document her recipe, my version here is entirely inspired by the way that my *yiayiá* would make them – using sugar to caramelize the red onion and grated carrot, and a pinch of cinnamon for aroma.

SERVES 4

200g (7oz) dried green lentils, rinsed and drained

185g (6½oz) long-grain rice

1 vegetable stock cube

3–4 tablespoons extra virgin olive oil

1 red onion, finely chopped

2 carrots, grated

1 teaspoon brown sugar

½ teaspoon ground cinnamon

2 bay leaves

Greek yogurt (10% fat), to serve

salt and pepper

1. Put the dried green lentils in a large saucepan with 1 litre (1¾ pints) of water. Place the pan over a medium heat and cook for 30 minutes until the lentils soften. Drain and set aside.

2. Meanwhile, in another saucepan, wash the rice, rinsing until the water runs clear. Drain then cover the rice in 370ml (13fl oz) of fresh water, add the stock cube and cook according to the packet instructions. Stir as the stock cube dissolves to ensure an even distribution of flavour.

3. Pour the oil into another large pan and place this over a medium heat. After a minute, add the onion and sauté for 2 minutes until it begins to soften. Add the carrot, sugar, cinnamon and bay leaves, and stir through to combine. Cook for a further 5 minutes until everything softens.

4. Add the drained lentils to the caramelized onions and carrots, together with the boiled rice. Season generously with salt and pepper and reduce the heat to low. Cover the pan with a lid and cook for another 5 minutes. If needed, stir through a little water and simmer until the texture of the *fakes* is completely soft.

5. Serve with Greek yogurt on the side.

FASOLÁKIA GIACHNÍ

Green Bean Stew

Fasolákia giachní is a simple green bean and potato stew cooked in a rich tomatoey sauce made using grated vine tomatoes, chopped canned tomatoes and tomato purée. It's unbelievably delicious because so much flavour comes from the tomato base, red onion and garlic. Just as it is, the stew is vegan but the dish is also brilliant with crumbled feta on top for an added salty kick – although this is optional.

SERVES 4

3 tablespoons extra virgin olive oil

1 red onion, finely chopped

2 garlic cloves, grated

500g (1lb 2oz) vine tomatoes, blitzed

50g (1¾oz) tomato purée

400g (14oz) can chopped tomatoes

700g (1lb 9oz) white potatoes, chopped into large chunks

400g (14oz) green beans, trimmed

500ml (18fl oz) water

salt and pepper

To serve (optional)

feta cheese, crumbled

flatbread (see page 57)

1. Pour the oil into a large saucepan and place over a medium–high heat. After a minute, add the finely chopped onion and stir through the oil. Sauté the onions for 2 minutes to soften them, then add the garlic, blitzed vine tomatoes and tomato purée, and stir until well combined. Cook for a further 5 minutes for the tomatoes to reduce and darken in colour, then add the canned tomatoes, potatoes and green beans. Mix everything together well.

2. Pour in enough of the hot water to cover the vegetables, season well with salt and pepper, and mix again.

3. Cover the pan with the lid and lower the heat to medium. Cook the stew for 30 minutes, checking and stirring through every 10 minutes to make sure that nothing sticks to the bottom.

4. If you wish, serve the stew with crumbled feta on top and flatbread on the side.

FASOLÁDA

Cannellini Bean Soup

Fasoláda is an incredibly hearty Greek soup made with cannellini beans that ooze in a rich, tomatoey sauce. The name comes from the word *fasoli*, which is Greek for bean. The traditional way is to soak dried cannellini beans overnight, but using canned beans reduces the total cooking time to under 30 minutes. It's a low-effort, packed-with-flavour and nutritious dish that you'll have on weekly rotation once you've tried it.

SERVES 3–4

2 tablespoons extra virgin olive oil

1 red onion, finely chopped

4 carrots, sliced

6 celery sticks, cut into chunks

50g (1¾oz) tomato purée

2 × 400g (14oz) cans cannellini beans, drained and rinsed

1 vegetable stock cube, dissolved in 500ml (18fl oz) hot water

2 bay leaves

salt and pepper

To garnish (optional)

finely chopped parsley

crumbled feta cheese

1. Pour the oil into a large saucepan and place over a high heat. After a minute, add the onion and stir through the oil. Sauté for 1 minute.

2. Reduce the heat to medium and add the carrots, celery and tomato purée. Stir to coat everything evenly in the purée and then cook for 5 minutes to release the flavour of the purée.

3. Add the cannellini beans along with the vegetable stock and bay leaves and stir again. Cover with a lid and leave to simmer for 20 minutes, stirring frequently.

4. Once the liquid has reduced and the vegetables have softened, remove the saucepan from the heat.

5. If you wish, stir through a little finely chopped parsley and serve with feta crumbled into each bowl.

REVYTHIÁ

Chickpea Stew

This hearty and comforting chickpea stew feels like a hug in a bowl when you're cold, hungry and can't be bothered to cook. It comes together in less than 30 minutes with a handful of staple ingredients. Instead of pre-soaking dried chickpeas overnight, I'm using good-quality canned ones for a quick but equally delicious soup, infused with bay leaves, dried oregano and a good squeeze of lemon juice for brightness. Enjoy this with a slice of bread on the side. Alternatively, serve the *revythiá* with my *tyrópsomo* (see page 158), and you'll be on to a winner.

SERVES 3

- 2 tablespoons extra virgin olive oil
- 1 large red onion, finely chopped
- 2 teaspoons dried oregano
- 2 bay leaves
- 2 carrots, chopped
- 2 × 400g (14oz) cans good-quality chickpeas, drained and rinsed
- 2 vegetable stock cubes, dissolved in 650ml (23fl oz) hot water
- juice of 1 lemon
- salt and pepper

1. Pour the oil into a large saucepan and place this over a medium heat. After a minute, add the onion, dried oregano and bay leaves, and stir through. Cook for about 2–3 minutes or until the onion has softened, then add the carrots and cook for a further 2–3 minutes.

2. Once the vegetables have softened, add the drained chickpeas and prepared vegetable stock to the pan, and reduce the heat. Cover with a lid and leave to simmer for 10 minutes, stirring a few times throughout.

3. Add the lemon juice and season generously with salt and pepper. Stir through and leave the soup to simmer for another minute until it thickens to your preferred consistency. Alternatively, if you would sooner have it runnier, stir in a little extra hot water.

4. Serve the *revythiá* warm with bread to soak up the juices.

EVERYDAY DINNERS LIKE A GREEK

SPANAKÓRIZO

Greek-style Spinach Risotto

Italy has risotto and Greece has *spanakórizo*, a silky spinach rice dish with spring onions and a generous amount of fresh dill and mint making it deliciously aromatic. Here, as in a *spanakópita* (Greek spinach pie), the earthy-flavoured spinach pairs perfectly with feta, which is crumbled on top before serving.

SERVES 4

2 tablespoons extra virgin olive oil

5 spring onions, chopped

30g (1oz) dill fronds, roughly chopped

30g (1oz) mint leaves, roughly chopped

250g (9oz) long-grain rice

1 vegetable stock cube, dissolved in 500ml (18fl oz) hot water

450g (1lb) fresh spinach, washed and drained

juice of ½ lemon

crumbled feta cheese, to serve (about 30g/1oz per serving)

salt and pepper

1 Pour the oil into a large saucepan and place over a medium heat. After a minute, add the chopped spring onions and herbs and stir through the oil. Sauté for 2–3 minutes until softened, stirring regularly.

2 Wash the rice, rinsing until the water runs clear, then drain. Add the rice and prepared vegetable stock to the pan, stir to combine, then cover with a lid and turn down the heat to low. Simmer for 15 minutes, until two-thirds of the liquid has been absorbed.

3 Next, incorporate the spinach. I add this in batches, stirring in a large handful of spinach and allowing it to wilt before adding the next batch. Repeat this until all of the spinach has been added to the rice, cover and cook over a low heat until all the liquid has fully been absorbed. This will take a further 15 minutes.

4 Once the rice has become silky in texture, pour in the lemon juice and season generously with salt and pepper. Stir to combine and serve the *spanakórizo* with crumbled feta on top.

MANÉSTRA

Orzo Stew

This hearty one-pot dish is enjoyed throughout Greece but its origins may lie in Corfu. *Manéstra* is essentially *kritharáki* (orzo) cooked in a rich tomatoey sauce. The choice of meat varies – I love to use beef for protein and texture and I stir through Parmesan at the end for a rich and silky finish. The fresh mint and parsley also give a final burst of flavour and balance this otherwise creamy dish.

SERVES 4

3 tablespoons extra virgin olive oil

1 red onion, finely chopped

2 carrots, finely chopped

2 celery sticks, finely chopped

250g (9oz) minced beef (5% fat)

½ teaspoon ground cinnamon

leaves from 2 fresh thyme sprigs, or 1 teaspoon dried thyme

1 teaspoon dried oregano

250g (9oz) orzo (or use macaroni – see tip)

500ml (18fl oz) passata

1 litre (1¾ pints) vegetable stock (see tip)

75g (2½oz) Parmesan cheese, grated

10g (¼oz) parsley, finely chopped

10g (¼oz) mint leaves, finely chopped

salt and pepper

1 Pour the oil into a large saucepan and place over a medium–high heat. After a minute, add the onion and sauté for 2 minutes until it begins to soften. Add the carrots and celery and cook for a further 5 minutes, stirring regularly throughout. Cover the pan with the lid so that the vegetables soften faster.

2 Add the minced beef to the pan and break it up using a wooden spoon. Brown the meat for 5 minutes. Add the cinnamon, thyme and oregano along with the orzo, passata and two-thirds of the prepared vegetable stock, and stir to combine.

3 Cook for 8–10 minutes, stirring regularly throughout, until the orzo softens and the sauce has reduced. Add the rest of the stock and lower the heat to simmer for 2–3 minutes. The consistency will be runny and almost soup-like.

4 Season with salt and pepper to taste and stir through the Parmesan, parsley and mint just before serving.

TOP TIP If you don't have orzo you can make this with 350g (12oz) macaroni instead, in which case only use 600ml (20fl oz) of vegetable stock, adding it all in one go at the same time as the passata.

KRITHARÁKI

Stovetop Tomato Orzo

Kritharáki is another one-pot orzo stew, except this one is vegetarian. Cooked in a rich tomatoey sauce with onion, *kritharáki* is satisfying as a meal in its own right but it also pairs perfectly with grilled or fried meats (like my *biftékia*, see page 114). I love to add grated halloumi at the end to coat the orzo and give it an ever richer, creamier consistency.

SERVES 4

2 tablespoons extra virgin olive oil, plus extra to serve

1 white onion, finely chopped

250g (9oz) orzo

500ml (18fl oz) passata

1 vegetable stock cube, dissolved in 500ml (18fl oz) hot water

50g (1¾oz) halloumi, grated

salt and pepper

1 Pour the oil into a large frying pan or saucepan and place over a medium heat. After a minute, add the onion and sauté for 2 minutes until it starts to soften. Once softened, add the orzo, passata, prepared vegetable stock and salt and pepper. Stir until everything is combined. Turn down the heat to low and cover the pan with a lid. Simmer for 12 minutes, stirring regularly throughout so that the orzo doesn't stick to the bottom of the pan.

2 Once the orzo is fully cooked and the sauce has thickened, stir through the grated halloumi and a drizzle of olive oil.

3 Serve the *kritharáki* warm as it is or with my *biftékia* (see page 114) or the Greek lemon chicken recipe on page 130.

BÁMIES LADERÉS

Okra Stew

For any okra-haters out there, my challenge is to convert you with *bámies laderés*! This is a super-tasty Greek vegetarian dish of okra cooked until meltingly tender in a rich tomatoey, garlicky sauce with lots of fresh dill and parsley. The preparation is simple yet the result is hearty and mouthwatering. I love to serve mine with an extra drizzle of olive oil and crumbled feta on top.

SERVES 4

5 tablespoons extra virgin olive oil

1 red onion, chopped

2 garlic cloves, finely chopped

750–800g (1lb 10–12oz) white potatoes (about 2 large ones), chopped

50g (1¾oz) tomato purée

1 vegetable stock cube, dissolved in 650ml (23fl oz) hot water

400g (14oz) can chopped tomatoes

500–550g (1lb 2–4oz) fresh okra, washed

60g (2¼oz) parsley, finely chopped

60g (2¼oz) dill fronds, finely chopped

salt and pepper

To serve (optional)

extra virgin olive oil

feta cheese, crumbled

chunky bread

1. Pour the oil into a large saucepan and place over a high heat. After a minute, add the onion and garlic to the pan and sauté for 2 minutes until they begin to soften. Then add the potatoes and tomato purée, mixing everything together. Leave to cook for a further 3–4 minutes until the purée darkens to a rich red.

2. Pour in the prepared vegetable stock and the tomatoes. Stir again then cover the pan with a lid and lower the heat to medium. Cook for 20 minutes, by which time the potatoes will have softened.

3. Trim off the stalks of the okra and add them to the pan, then stir again and make sure all the okra are submerged in the tomatoey sauce, so that they cook evenly. Place the lid back on the pan and cook for a further 12–15 minutes.

4. After this time, remove the stew from the heat and stir through the parsley and dill, then season with salt and pepper to taste. Place the lid back on the pan and leave the stew to settle for a few minutes.

5. If you wish, serve the stew with a drizzle of extra virgin olive oil and a little feta crumbled on top and chunky bread on the side.

PLIGOÚRI

Tomatoey Bulgur Wheat

Pligoúri, or *pourgouri* as it's known in Cyprus, is a bulgur wheat pilaf dish cooked in a base of beef tomatoes and red onion that are grated or finely chopped for maximum flavour. It's a hearty and naturally plant-based dish that has a satisfying silky texture from the combination of fine bulgur wheat and broken vermicelli. I grew up eating *pligoúri* with a spoonful of Greek yogurt on the side, which works so well with its tomatoey flavour. I also absolutely love serving this with my *biftékia* recipe (see page 114) – or any grilled or roasted meat. It comes together in less than 30 minutes and there's minimal preparation, making it a perfect meal for busy weeknights.

SERVES 3–4

2 tablespoons extra virgin Greek olive oil

1 red onion, grated or finely chopped

4 beef tomatoes, grated or blitzed in a food processor

1 tablespoon tomato purée

60g (2¼oz) broken vermicelli

100g (3½oz) fine bulgur wheat

500ml (18fl oz) hot water

Greek yogurt (10% fat), to serve (optional)

salt and pepper

1 Pour the oil into a saucepan and place over a medium heat. After a minute add the onion and cook for 2 minutes, stirring regularly until softened. Pour in the tomatoes and add the tomato purée. Stir and cook for another 2–3 minutes to allow them to darken in colour and the liquid to reduce.

2 Add in the broken vermicelli, bulgur wheat and measured water, and stir until everything is well incorporated. Partially cover the pan with a lid and turn down the heat to low.

3 Leave to cook for 10–12 minutes until the liquid reduces and the texture is silky. Remove the lid from the saucepan and season to taste.

4 Serve warm with a spoonful of yogurt if you wish. *Pligoúri* keeps in the fridge for up to 2 days in an airtight container.

GÁRIDES SAGANÁKI

Pan-fried Prawns in Tomato Sauce

Prawns cooked in a garlicky, tomatoey sauce are traditionally served as an appetizer in Greece but can also be enjoyed as a meal. For the tastiest result, use uncooked king prawns instead of cooked ones. The special ingredient in the tomato sauce here is the anise liqueur ouzo, which gives it real depth of flavour. Top off the prawns with lots of fresh parsley and crumbled feta, and you're on to a weeknight winner.

SERVES 2–3

2–3 tablespoons extra virgin olive oil

330g (11½oz) uncooked, shell-off king prawns (allow about 8 per serving)

1 red onion, chopped

2 sweet pointed peppers, stems and seeds removed, chopped

400g (14oz) can chopped tomatoes

30g (1oz) tomato purée

3 garlic cloves, grated

4 teaspoons ouzo (optional)

¼–½ teaspoon chilli flakes

1 teaspoon smoked paprika

10g (¼oz) parsley, chopped

100g (3½oz) feta cheese, crumbled

salt and pepper

1 Pour 2 tablespoons of the oil into a large frying pan and place over a high heat. After a minute, add the prawns, one by one, and cook on each side for no more than a minute, or until pink. Remove from the pan and set aside on a plate.

2 Once all the prawns have been cooked, add the onion and pepper to the same pan and cook for 5 minutes over a low heat until softened – you may need to add the remaining oil. Add the tomatoes, tomato purée, garlic, ouzo (if using), chilli, paprika, salt and pepper. Cook over a high heat for a further 5 minutes until the sauce has reduced and thickened, and the smell of the ouzo has dissipated.

3 Return the prawns to the pan and stir them through the sauce. Lower the heat and leave to simmer for a final minute before removing the pan from the heat.

4 Top the *saganáki* with the parsley, crumble over the feta and enjoy warm.

BIFTÉKIA

Beef Patties

SERVES 4

1 large red onion, grated or finely chopped

30g (1oz) parsley, chopped

30g (1oz) mint leaves, chopped

1 medium egg

100g (3½oz) breadcrumbs

500g (1lb 2oz) minced beef (20% fat)

1 teaspoon dried oregano

olive oil for shallow-frying (just enough to come one-third of the way up the sides of the burger patties) or air-frying

salt and pepper

Biftékia are meat patties and get their name from the word *biftéki*, meaning hamburger in Greek. Every time I've shared my recipe online it's taken people by storm. The *biftékia* are juicy and flavoursome thanks to the red onion and plenty of freshly chopped herbs. They come together in less than 30 minutes and, once you try them, you'll never want to go back to eating ordinary burgers again. Here you have the recipe for frying the patties and the healthier option of air-frying, and opposite is a variation for making them as gyros.

1 Put the onion in a large mixing bowl with the parsley and mint.

2 Add the egg, breadcrumbs, minced beef and seasonings to the bowl and mix until well combined. I do this by hand, wearing disposable gloves, making it easier to combine the ingredients without overworking the meat.

3 Take about a tablespoonful of the mixture and flatten it in the palm of your hand to a thickness of 1–1.5cm (½–⅝ inch). Then round off the edges to form a burger or patty shape. Repeat this process with the remaining mixture to make 12.

4 If frying the patties, pour enough oil into a large frying pan to a depth of about 4mm (¼ inch) and place over a high heat. After 2 minutes, or once the oil is hot enough (check by sticking the tip of a wooden spoon in the pan to see if the oil bubbles up around it), carefully place the patties in the pan, leaving enough room between each one to allow them to cook evenly – you may need to cook the patties in batches.

5 Shallow-fry the *biftékia* for 3–4 minutes on each side until they are crispy and golden. Transfer the cooked batch to a plate lined with kitchen paper to absorb any excess oil. Repeat with the rest.

6 Serve the *biftékia* warm. I recommend enjoying them with tzatziki (see page 23), flatbread (see page 57) and a side of *maroulosaláta* (see page 83).

AIR FRYER

For a healthier cooking option that requires far less oil, you can air-fry the shaped *biftékia* instead of shallow-frying. To do this, put 1 tablespoon of oil in the air-fryer tray. Place half the patties in the tray, leaving space between each one. Air-fry at 180°C (350°F) for 12 minutes, turning the *biftékia* halfway through. Repeat with the remaining patties. You won't need to add more oil to the tray for the second batch.

VARIATION: BIFTÉKIA GÝROS

Beef Patties in Gyros Form

For a hands-off kind of dinner that you can whack straight in the oven, you can also create a gyros which, once carved, turns into gorgeous crispy bits that you can stuff into pitta bread. You need a kebab spike to make gyros but you can easily create a makeshift one (see the tip for my chicken gyros recipe, page 133).

SERVES 4

1 × quantity of prepared *biftékia* mixture (see recipe opposite)

1 onion, halved

1 Preheat the oven to 150°C fan (345°F), Gas Mark 3½ and line a baking tray with baking paper. Prepare the *biftékia* mixture as opposite. Place a kebab spike on the lined tray and skewer with one of the onion halves to make the base. Using your hands, mould about a handful of the mixture around the base of the spike so that it sticks. Repeat this with the rest of the mixture, a handful at a time, and moulding it around the kebab spike to build up your gyros. Then skewer the other onion half on top.

2 Cover the gyros with foil and place it in the oven to bake for 2¼ hours. Remove the foil about 30 minutes before the end of the cooking time to allow the outside to become crispy. Transfer to a board, pull out the kebab spike and carefully carve the gyros into thin strips. You could also carve the gyros when you remove the foil and return the shavings to the oven to crisp up more evenly.

3 Serve the gyros on flatbread (see page 57) with tzatziki (see page 23) and some thinly sliced tomato and red onion.

SOUVLÁKI ARNÍ

Lamb Souvlaki

Souvlaki are skewers of grilled meat and lamb souvlaki is the best kind out there, in my humble opinion! Diced lamb is marinated in a lemony, garlicky yogurt base then grilled or fried until tender on the inside and crispy and golden on the outside. I find shoulder more tender than leg but you can use either cut. The best way to serve any souvlaki, is encased in pitta bread (see page 58–60) with a generous helping of tzatziki (see page 23).

MAKES 4 SKEWERS/ SERVES 2

400g (14oz) diced shoulder or leg of lamb

For the marinade

100g (3½oz) Greek yogurt (10% fat)

1½ tablespoons extra virgin olive oil

juice of 2 lemons

2 teaspoons dried oregano

1 teaspoon dried mint

½ teaspoon dried thyme

½ teaspoon ground cumin

½ teaspoon ground coriander

3 garlic cloves, grated or crushed

½ teaspoon ground black pepper

salt to taste

1 Put all the marinade ingredients in a large, non-metallic bowl and mix well to combine. Add the diced lamb to the marinade and mix to coat everything evenly. Cover the bowl and refrigerate for 2 hours.

2 Meanwhile, if using wooden skewers, place them on a tray and soak them in water, which stops them from burning.

3 Once the meat has marinated, thread 8–10 pieces on to each skewer, or roughly divide the amount by 4.

4 Place a griddle pan or frying pan over a medium–high heat. After 1–2 minutes, place the skewers on the hot pan and cook them for 5 minutes on both sides until lightly charred.

5 Remove the meat from the skewers and serve warm in pitta bread (see pages 58–60) with tzatziki (see page 23). I like *horiátiki saláta* (see page 78) as a side.

Feast
e a
Greek

5. Feas

For times when you need meals made in large quantities, here are my labour-of-love, well-worth-the-wait dishes that form the centrepiece at social gatherings. Take your pick: from **moussaka** to **pastítsio** (Greek lasagne) or **gemistá** (stuffed peppers and tomatoes) and – my all-time favourite – **kléftiko**, marinated, slow-cooked lamb, which, after years of retesting, I've recreated in the way that I remember having in Greece. You'll also find my legendary **chicken gyros** for those occasions where you want to create your own Greek feast. It's a total crowd-pleaser, one that I've made for parties of more than 20 guests, and pairs perfectly with my tzatziki and flatbread recipes. Even if you're not hosting, there are dishes that you'll come back to again and again – like **avgolémono**, a popular Greek chicken and rice soup served with a lemony egg broth, and a **Greek lemon chicken** that I could never get bored of.

AVGOLÉMONO

Lemony Chicken and Rice Soup

Avgolémono really is the best thing since sliced bread, for a very good reason. This simple chicken and rice soup, made with a lemony egg broth, single-handedly cures me whenever I'm feeling run down. So, I've got you covered whenever you're in need of a pick-me-up. My recipe calls for a whole chicken for maximum flavour for the broth, as well as lemon zest, which really lifts this soup. Besides being comforting, *Avgolémono* is also made to break fast during the Orthodox Easter. I have such fond memories of enjoying it with family after midnight mass, so it has a special place in my heart.

SERVES 4

1 corn-fed poussin, weighing about 500g (1lb 2oz)

2 chicken stock cubes, dissolved in 1 litre (1¾ pints) hot water

120g (4oz) long-grain rice

600ml (20fl oz) hot water

2 large eggs

zest of 1 lemon and juice of 2

olive oil, for drizzling (optional)

salt and pepper

1 Put the chicken in a large saucepan and pour in the prepared stock. Cover with a lid and place the pan over a high heat. Cook the chicken for 35 minutes until it's fork tender, turning it over halfway through.

2 Transfer the chicken to a large plate or board and shred it with a knife and fork, removing all the bones and most of the fat. Return the shredded meat to the pan and turn the heat to low.

3 Wash the rice, rinsing until the water runs clear, then drain and add to the pan. Cook for 12 minutes, stirring regularly. The stock will reduce, so at this point add the measured water.

4 Crack the eggs into a bowl and, while whisking, slowly incorporate the lemon juice until the mixture becomes frothy. Whisk in the zest too.

5 Once the rice has cooked, add the beaten egg mixture to the pan and stir. Cook for a further 2–3 minutes until the consistency has thickened. Taste and season with salt and pepper.

6 Serve warm, drizzled with a little olive oil if liked. The *avgolémono* will thicken further as it cools down, so add more hot water to the soup if you'd like it to be thinner.

SALANTOURMÁSI

Stuffed Onions

SERVES 8–10

6 large white onions

For the filling

2 tablespoons extra virgin olive oil

2 red onions, finely chopped

2 garlic cloves, crushed or grated

15g (½oz) tomato purée

500g (1lb 2oz) minced beef (20% fat)

250g (9oz) long-grain rice

400g (14oz) vine tomatoes

1 beef stock cube

40g (1½oz) parsley, finely chopped

40g (1½oz) dill fronds, finely chopped

15g (½oz) mint leaves, finely chopped

salt and pepper

For the sauce

500ml (18fl oz) passata

1 tablespoon balsamic vinegar

1 tablespoon extra virgin olive oil

These tender, flavour-packed onion morsels are made with the most aromatic and delicious stuffing of rice, mince and fresh herbs. Wrapped to form dumpling-like shapes, these twice-cooked stuffed onions are soft, tender, even a little bit sweet, which perfectly balances the herby filling. They're smothered in a passata sauce then baked until gorgeously tender. Enjoy on their own or as part of a mezze.

1 Start by chopping both ends off the white onions and then peeling them. Then make a slit down one side of each one, cutting through to the centre. Place the onions in a large saucepan with enough water to cover, put the lid on and boil over a medium heat for 15 minutes until softened. Remove the onions from the pan with a slotted spoon and transfer to a bowl to cool. Reserve the onion cooking water.

2 Next, prepare the filling. Pour the oil into another large saucepan and place over a high heat. After a minute, add the onion and sauté for 2 minutes until softened. Then add the garlic and tomato purée and cook for 2 minutes more until the purée darkens.

3 Lower the heat to medium and add the minced beef, roughly breaking it into chunks with a wooden spoon and cook for 5–7 minutes, stirring regularly to ensure it browns evenly.

4 Meanwhile, wash the rice, rinsing until the water runs clear, then drain. Add the tomatoes to a food processor and blitz to a pulp.

5 Add the rice, beef stock cube, 250ml (9fl oz) of the reserved onion water and the blitzed tomatoes to the pan. Stir to combine then cover the pan and leave to cook for 5 minutes, before stirring again then cook, covered, for a further 5 minutes. The stock will reduce, and the tomatoes will become soft and jammy. Stir through the herbs, season, then take the pan off the heat. The rice will be al dente, which is as intended, and will cook fully in due course.

6 Select two baking dishes (mine are 25 × 32cm/10 × 12½ inches) and preheat the oven to 180°C fan (400°F), Gas Mark 6.

7 To stuff the onions, peel a layer from one and place a heaped tablespoon of the mince rice filling in the centre. Then roll from the bottom up to wrap the filling and seal the stuffed onion. Repeat this process with the remaining onions and filling, lining up the *salantourmási* in three or four rows in the baking dishes.

8 To prepare the sauce, simply put the ingredients in a large jug with 100ml (3½fl oz) of the reserved onion water. Season with salt and pepper and stir to combine. Pour the sauce over the stuffed onions, dividing the amount evenly between the two dishes.

9 Cover the dishes with foil and bake for 40 minutes, removing the foil for the final 10 minutes to allow the tops of the *salantourmási* to become a bit crispy. Serve warm with a side of olives and crusty bread.

KIMADÓPITA

Filo Meat Pie

Kimadópita consists of a rich minced beef filling sandwiched between layers of buttery, crispy filo pastry. It's unlike any meat pie I've had before. The grated cheese melts into the minced beef, giving the *kimadópita* its distinct depth of flavour. If you can't find Kasseri cheese use Parmigiano Reggiano instead. *Kimadópita* can be served as a main – just divide the pie into bigger portions – or as a snack, once chilled.

SERVES 3–4

2 tablespoons extra virgin olive oil, plus extra for brushing

1 white onion, chopped

2 carrots, chopped

1–2 celery sticks, chopped

500g (1lb 2oz) minced beef (5% fat)

1 vegetable stock cube, mixed with 250ml (9fl oz) hot water

125ml (4fl oz) red wine

60g (2¼oz) tomato purée

2 teaspoons dried oregano

1 teaspoon dried thyme

50g (1¾oz) Kasseri cheese, grated, or substitute with Parmigiano Reggiano

200g (7oz) filo pastry (6–8 sheets)

salt and pepper

1 Pour the oil into a large frying pan and place over a high heat. After a minute, add the onion, carrots and celery and sauté for 5 minutes until softened, stirring regularly throughout. Add the minced beef, breaking it into chunks with the back of a spoon, and cook for a further 5 minutes, until it has browned evenly.

2 Stir in the prepared vegetable stock, wine, tomato purée and dried herbs. Season with salt and pepper and continue cooking for another 5 minutes, or until the sauce has reduced and thickened. Stir through the grated cheese until it's melted into the meat sauce.

3 Preheat the oven to 180°C fan (400°F), Gas Mark 6. Brush a couple of teaspoons of oil over the base and sides of a 23cm (9 inch) square baking dish. Line with 3 or 4 sheets of filo, cut to the size of the pan, and brush more olive oil on top. Pour in the meat filling and spread out in an even layer. Top with another 3 or 4 sheets of filo and brush more oil over the top.

4 Using a sharp knife, carefully cut the *kimadópita* into the required number of portions then bake for 25–30 minutes until it's golden on top. Leave to cool for 10 minutes before serving.

KOTÓPOULO LEMONÁTO STO FOURNÓ

Greek Lemon Chicken

I will never get bored of chicken cooked like this – I grew up eating it this way and it's how I'll continue! A simple combination of lemon juice, olive oil, oregano and salt and pepper makes for incredibly tender and flavoursome chicken. I recommend using poussins for their tender meat. I love serving these with *kritharáki* (see page 108) or roast potatoes.

SERVES 4

2 poussins, weighing 1kg (2lb 4oz) in total

For the marinade

juice of 3 lemons

6 tablespoons extra virgin olive oil

2 teaspoons dried oregano

½ teaspoon ground black pepper

2 teaspoons salt, or to taste

1 Preheat the oven to 180°C fan (400°F), Gas Mark 6. Spatchcock the 2 chickens by placing them breast-side down on a flat surface. Using a sharp knife, cut along either side of the backbone to open up the carcass. Lay the flattened birds side by side in a large roasting tray.

2 Make the marinade by stirring together the ingredients in a jar. Pour half over the spatchcocked birds, flip the chickens over, then pour the rest of the marinade over the other side. Cover the tray with a sheet of foil and bake for 45 minutes.

3 After this time, remove the foil and increase the temperature to 200°C fan (425°F), Gas Mark 7. Return the tray to the oven and cook the chickens for a further 12–15 minutes until golden brown on top.

4 Carve the 2 chickens, cutting off the thighs, drumsticks, breasts and wings as portions, and serve.

GÝROS KOTÓPOULO

Chicken Gyros

I proudly call this the best homemade chicken gyros recipe out there. Served countless times for friends and family at dinner parties, this recipe has been loved by all who have tried it. Gyros is incredibly simple to make – you just need to allow a few hours to marinate the chicken thighs for maximum flavour then skewer them on to a kebab spike. As with all gyros, the shavings of meat are traditionally served on a bed of flatbread and tzatziki, then loaded with chips, tomatoes and sliced red onion.

SERVES SERVES 4

600g (1lb 5oz) skinless, boneless chicken thigh fillets

For the marinade

250g (9oz) Greek yogurt (10% fat)

juice of ½ lemon

2 garlic cloves, crushed

1 teaspoon ground cumin

1 teaspoon ground coriander

½ teaspoon ground cinnamon

2 heaped teaspoons dried oregano

½ teaspoon smoked paprika

2 tablespoons extra virgin olive oil

salt and pepper

For the kebab spike (see tip)

1 red onion, halved

1 Place the chicken thighs in a large, non-metallic bowl and add all the marinade ingredients. Mix everything until the chicken is evenly coated, cover and refrigerate for at least 2 hours.

2 Preheat the oven to 170°C fan (375°F), Gas Mark 5. To prepare the gyros, line a large baking tray with baking paper. Place the kebab spike on top and spear with a red onion half for the base then pierce the marinated thighs, threading them on the spike one on top of the other. Top off with the other red onion half.

3 Coat the gyros with the remaining marinade and cook for 50–55 minutes, or until the juices run clear and the top of the gyros is slightly charred.

4 Using a carving knife, carefully carve the gyros (still on the spike is easier, especially at first) into thin shavings and transfer all the meat to a serving plate, pouring all the juices over.

5 Serve in the traditional way: on flatbreads (see page 57) with tzatziki (see page 23), chips and sliced tomatoes and red onions.

TOP TIP If you don't have a kebab spike, you can easily create a makeshift one by cutting an onion in half, placing 2 halves, cut side down, on the lined tray, and spearing one of the halves with 2 wooden skewers. Assemble the gyros by piercing the chicken thighs, threading them on the skewers one on top of the other, and top the gyros with the remaining onion half.

GÝROS CHOIRINÓS

Pork Gyros

Pork gyros is another classic, enjoyed all over Greece. Pork shoulder steaks marinate in a gorgeous garlicky and oniony yogurt base before being skewered on to a kebab spike, layered between slices of red onion that soften and sweeten as the gyros slow-cooks until slightly charred on top yet perfectly juicy and tender in the middle. It is an absolute flavour bomb with a spice blend – different from my chicken gyros – chosen to complement the pork.

SERVES 4–6

700g (1lb 9oz) pork shoulder steaks, cut into chunks if necessary

½ red onion, thinly sliced

For the marinade

3 tablespoons extra virgin olive oil

1½ tablespoons white wine vinegar

100g (3½oz) Greek yogurt (10% fat)

2 teaspoons dried oregano

1 teaspoon ground cumin

1 teaspoon smoked paprika

2 garlic cloves, grated

1 teaspoon Dijon mustard

½ teaspoon ground black pepper

2 teaspoons salt, or to taste

For the kebab spike
(see my tip under Chicken Gyros, page 133, for creating a makeshift one)

1 red onion, halved

1 Put all the marinade ingredients in a large, non-metallic bowl and mix to combine. Add the pork and onion to the bowl and mix again to coat everything evenly in the marinade. Cover the bowl and refrigerate for at least 2 hours.

2 Preheat the oven to 150°C fan (345°F), Gas Mark 3½. To prepare the gyros, line a large baking tray with baking paper. Place the kebab spike on top and spear with an onion half for the base then pierce the marinated pork steaks, threading them alternately with the red onion slices, one on top of the other. Top off the gyros with the other onion half.

3 Wrap the gyros in 2 sheets of foil, tucking in the sides as best as possible to trap in the heat, as this will tenderize the pork. Cook for 2½ hours then remove the foil, increase the temperature to 200°C fan (425°F), Gas Mark 7, and cook for 10–15 minutes until golden brown and crisp on top.

4 Using a carving knife, carefully carve the gyros (still on the spike is easier, especially at first) into thin shavings and transfer all the meat to a serving plate, pouring all the juices over, and serve.

GEMISTÁ

Stuffed Peppers and Tomatoes

I grew up watching my *yiayiá* (grandma) make *gemistá* – peppers and tomatoes stuffed with the most flavoursome minced beef and rice filling – and recreating this dish brings back so many fond memories. This dish requires a little patience as you bake the stuffed veg low and slow until tender and slightly charred.

SERVES 6

9 large peppers
6 large vine tomatoes

For the filling

3 tablespoons extra virgin olive oil, plus extra for drizzling
2 red onions, finely chopped
2 garlic cloves, crushed or grated
15g (½oz) tomato purée
500g (1lb 2oz) minced beef (20% fat)
250g (9oz) long-grain rice
1 beef stock cube dissolved in 250ml (9fl oz) hot water
15g (½oz) mint leaves, finely chopped
40g (1½oz) parsley, finely chopped
40g (1½oz) dill fronds, finely chopped
salt and pepper

1 Cut the tops off the peppers, roughly 2.5cm (1 inch) below the stem, and scoop out any membrane and seeds. Next, cut a thin slice from the core end of the tomatoes and carefully scrape the juice, flesh and seeds into a bowl and set aside for later. Arrange the pepper and tomato shells upright in a large (30 × 40cm/ 12 × 16 inch) baking tray, reserving the tops.

2 To prepare the filling, heat the oil in a large saucepan over a high heat. Add the onions and sauté for 2 minutes until softened. Add the garlic and tomato purée and cook for a further 2 minutes or until the purée darkens. Lower the heat to medium and add the minced beef, breaking it up into chunks with a wooden spoon. Cook for 5–7 minutes, stirring regularly, to ensure it browns evenly.

3 Wash the rice, rinsing until the water runs clear, then drain. Add the rice, prepared beef stock and reserved tomato flesh to the saucepan and stir to combine. Cover the pan and leave to cook for 5 minutes, then stir again, cover and cook for a further 5 minutes until the stock has reduced and the tomato flesh is soft and jammy. At this point, stir through the chopped fresh herbs and take the pan off the heat. The rice will be al dente, which is as intended.

4 Preheat the oven to 150°C fan (345°F), Gas Mark 3½. Stuff each pepper and tomato to the brim with the mince and rice filling. Put the stuffed veg back in the tray, keeping them upright, and place their tops back on. Drizzle over extra oil, season and pour 250ml (9fl oz) of hot water into the baking tray. Cover the entire tray with foil (you may need 2 sheets to ensure it's covered fully), and tuck in the sides. Bake for 2 hours. Uncover the tray, increase the oven temperature to 200°C fan (425°F), Gas Mark 7 and bake the *gemistá* for a final 10–15 minutes until golden. Serve as they are, or with a chunk of feta on the side.

KÉIK DOLMADÁKI

Dolma Cake

SERVES 8–10

160–170g (about 6oz) vine leaves in brine, drained, stalks removed

1 tablespoon extra virgin olive oil

250ml (9fl oz) hot water

For the filling

3 tablespoons extra virgin olive oil

2 red onions, finely chopped

2 garlic cloves, crushed

30g (1oz) tomato purée

500g (1lb 2oz) minced beef (20% fat)

250g (9oz) long-grain rice

450g (1lb) vine tomatoes

1 beef stock cube dissolved in 500ml (18fl oz) hot water

15g (½oz) mint leaves, finely chopped

60g (2¼oz) parsley, finely chopped

60g (2¼oz) dill fronds, finely chopped

salt and pepper

Introducing what I like to call a dolma cake, for those who love *dolmadákia* (see page 55) but don't want the bother of making individually stuffed vine leaves! Here you simply make a mince and rice filling using fresh tomatoes for maximum flavour, and line the bottom of a saucepan with vine leaves to create the base. Add the filling, top it off and seal the edges with more vine leaves, then simmer until it's fully cooked. The result: a textured top that's reminiscent of crispy seaweed, and a tender filling that you can simply slice up and serve like cake.

1 To prepare the filling, pour the oil into a large saucepan and place over a high heat. After a minute, add the onions and sauté for 2 minutes until they soften and become translucent. Stir in the garlic and tomato purée and cook for a further 2 minutes until the purée darkens.

2 Reduce the heat to medium and add the minced beef, roughly breaking it up into chunks with a wooden spoon and cook for 5–7 minutes, stirring regularly to ensure it browns evenly.

3 Meanwhile, wash the rice, rinsing until the water runs clear, then drain. Blitz the vine tomatoes in a food processor to a pulp, or you can simply grate them by hand, discarding the skins.

4 Add the rice, prepared beef stock and tomato pulp and stir to combine. Cover the pan with a lid and leave to cook for 5 minutes, before stirring again then cooking, covered, for a final 5 minutes. The stock will reduce and the tomatoes will become soft and jammy.

5 Stir through the chopped fresh herbs and take the pan off the heat. The rice will be al dente, which is as intended as it will cook fully in due course.

6 Rinse the vine leaves for about 30 seconds under cold water to remove the flavour of the brine then set them aside in a colander to drain completely. Grease the base and sides of a deep saucepan with the oil then line the base with a layer of vine leaves, spreading them out completely. Repeat this process with the sides of the pan, forming a layer of vine leaves all round and overlapping them slightly with the bottom layer. Aim to cover about a quarter of the pan's depth to give enough height to the dolma cake. Carefully add the filling to the pan, spreading it evenly to cover the base and side layers of vine leaves. Use the remaining vine leaves to cover the top completely, tucking the leaves in around the sides to seal the cake. Pour over the measured hot water and place a side plate, upside down, on top of the dolma cake, to weigh down the top. Cover the pan with a lid and place over a medium heat.

7 Cook the dolma cake for a total of 1 hour. After 35 minutes, remove the lid of the pan and continue to cook, uncovered, for the remaining 25 minutes. Then, 10 minutes before the hour is up, take the pan off the heat and carefully remove the side plate. (I use 2 tablespoons on each side to lift it and, once I'm able to grip the plate, I use oven gloves to set it aside.) Return the pan to the heat, uncovered, for the final 10 minutes – the remaining liquid in the pan will reduce completely. Set aside to cool for 30 minutes.

8 Run a spatula around the dolma cake a few times to release it from the sides of the pan. Place a large plate over the top (at least as large as the pan) and carefully invert it so that the cake drops on to the plate. Leave to cool for at least an hour before slicing and serving.

PASTÍTSIO

Greek Lasagne

SERVES 10

500g (1lb 2oz) bucatini (a tube pasta specifically used for *pastítsio*)

For the mince sauce

3 tablespoons extra virgin olive oil

1 red onion, finely chopped

1 teaspoon fresh thyme leaves

1 teaspoon fresh oregano, finely chopped

1 garlic clove, crushed

50g (1¾oz) tomato purée

500g (1lb 2oz) minced pork (5% fat)

500g (1lb 2oz) minced beef (10% fat)

400g (14oz) can chopped tomatoes

125ml (4fl oz) red wine

2 beef stock cubes dissolved in 250ml (9fl oz) hot water

2 bay leaves

1 teaspoon ground cinnamon, plus extra to garnish

50–60g (1¾–2¼oz) parsley, finely chopped

salt and pepper

For the béchamel

120g (4oz) butter

150g (5½oz) plain flour

1.35 litres (2¼ pints) full-fat milk

1 egg yolk

100g (3½oz) Parmesan cheese, grated

½ teaspoon grated nutmeg

To assemble

extra virgin olive oil, for greasing

70g (2½oz) Parmesan cheese, grated

Pastítsio – or *makarónia tou foúrnou* as it's known in Cyprus – is a decadent and impressive-looking layered pasta dish that, when cooled, becomes even more delicious. A specific kind of bucatini, a tube pasta resembling thick spaghetti and recognized by Greeks as 'the pasta to use for *pastítsio*', forms the base. The dish is layered with a rich tomato and meat sauce then topped with a creamy béchamel. *Pastítsio* is comfort food at its finest and every mouthful makes the labour of love worthwhile.

1 First make the sauce. Pour the oil into a large saucepan and place over a medium–high heat. After a minute, stir in the onion and sauté for 2 minutes until it begins to soften. Add the thyme, oregano, garlic and tomato purée and stir again. Cook for a further 2–3 minutes until the purée deepens in colour.

2 Add the minced meats to the pan and roughly break up into chunks with a wooden spoon to incorporate with the tomatoey base. Cook for about 10 minutes or until the meat is evenly browned.

3 Stir in the tomatoes, wine, prepared stock, bay leaves and cinnamon. Turn down the heat to medium and cover the pan with a lid. Cook for about 20 minutes, stirring occasionally, by which time the sauce will have thickened and the smell of the wine will have dissipated. Remove the bay leaves from the sauce and set the pan aside.

4 Next, prepare the béchamel. Melt the butter in another large saucepan over a medium heat. Once it has melted, add the flour and whisk: it will form a thick roux. Slowly add the milk in 5–6 goes (about 200ml/7fl oz at a time), whisking continuously to stop any clumps forming, until the sauce thickens. Once all the milk has been added, add the egg yolk, Parmesan and nutmeg, whisking again to combine until the cheese has melted and the consistency is silky smooth. Remove from the heat.

FEAST LIKE A GREEK

5 Add a ladle's worth of the béchamel to the mince sauce – this creates an even richer texture. Then stir the parsley into the meat sauce. Set aside.

6 Preheat the oven to 180°C fan (400°F), Gas Mark 6.

7 Meanwhile, cook the bucatini in a large pan of boiling salted water for 2–3 minutes less than the packet instructions so that the pasta doesn't become soggy and overcooked when baked in the *pastítsio*. Drain.

8 To assemble the *pastítsio*, I recommend using a large, deep-sided baking tray (about 30 × 40cm/12 × 16 inches). Start by greasing the base with about 2 tablespoons of oil (to prevent the pasta from sticking), then toss in the al dente bucatini and spread it out to fill the tray. Add the mince sauce and spread over the pasta. Spoon in the béchamel to form a layer over the mince sauce. Smooth carefully with a spatula, trying to avoid blending the béchamel with the meat layer. Finally, top the béchamel with the grated Parmesan and a light dusting of cinnamon. Bake for 40 minutes until beautifully golden on top.

9 Leave the *pastítsio* to cool for at least an hour before slicing and serving – this keeps the layers intact.

SOUTZOUKÁKIA

Baked Meatballs

SERVES 4–6

For the meatballs

300g (10½oz) white bread, torn into pieces

3 garlic cloves

handful of mint leaves

1 red onion

1½ teaspoons ground cumin

1 teaspoon ground cinnamon

¼ teaspoon chilli flakes

500g (1lb 2oz) minced beef (20% fat)

500g (1lb 2oz) minced pork (5% fat)

1 egg

about 3 teaspoons salt

about 1 teaspoon ground black pepper

150g (5½oz) plain flour, for dredging

300ml (10fl oz) sunflower oil, for frying

For the sauce

1 red onion, chopped

2 tablespoons caster sugar

2 × 400g (14oz) cans chopped tomatoes

½ teaspoon ground cinnamon

3 bay leaves

2 chicken stock cubes, dissolved in 500ml (18fl oz) hot water

These oblong-shaped meatballs share their roots with the Turkish spicy meatball dish called *İzmir köfte*. They are packed full of flavour from cumin, cinnamon and chilli flakes, with fresh mint for brightness. *Soutzoukákia* are shallow-fried until golden brown and crispy then covered in a tomato sauce, infused with a touch more cinnamon and baked until tender. For me, these are the ultimate meatballs – you'll keep coming back for more.

1 Start by preparing the meatballs. Blitz the bread pieces in a food processor for about a minute to make fresh breadcrumbs (don't worry if a few chunkier bits remain). Tip the breadcrumbs into a large mixing bowl.

2 Add the garlic, mint leaves, red onion, cumin, cinnamon and chilli flakes to the food processor. Blitz until a paste forms. Add this to the bowl of breadcrumbs, along with the minced meats, egg and a generous seasoning of salt and pepper (I've given my recommended amounts). Mix by hand, wearing disposable gloves if you wish, to ensure the seasonings and breadcrumbs are well incorporated into the meat.

3 Set up 3 plates. Put the flour on one; the second is for placing the prepared meatballs; and line the third with kitchen paper, ready for absorbing excess oil from the fried meatballs. Take a heaped tablespoon of the meatball mixture and shape into an oval. Dredge in the flour and set aside on the second plate. Repeat with the rest to make about 20 meatballs.

4 Add the sunflower oil to a large frying pan and place over a high heat. To check the oil is hot enough, stick the tip of a wooden spoon in the pan to see if the oil bubbles up around it. Add the meatballs to the pan, one at a time, without overcrowding it; if they don't all fit at once, cook them in batches. Brown the meatballs for 2–3 minutes on both sides.

5 Remove the meatballs from the frying pan and place on the plate lined with kitchen paper.

6 Use the same pan to make the sauce. Reserve 2 tablespoons of the cooking oil and drain off the rest. Place the pan over a medium heat, add the onion and sugar, and sauté for 2 minutes, stirring regularly, until the onion caramelizes. Stir in the tomatoes, cinnamon, bay leaves and prepared chicken stock. Lower the heat and simmer for 10–12 minutes until the sauce reduces.

7 Meanwhile preheat the oven to 170°C fan (375°F), Gas Mark 5. Put the meatballs in a large roasting tray and pour over the sauce – make sure they are all covered. Bake for 40 minutes.

8 Serve warm with basmati rice or pitta bread (see pages 58–60) to soak up all the delicious sauce.

PATÁTES LEMONÁTES

Lemony Roast Potatoes

Lemony, garlicky Greek roast potatoes are the ultimate accompaniment to any roast meat or fish. That said, they're so delicious, you can enjoy them just as they are! Coated in plenty of olive oil, lemon juice and seasoned generously with dried oregano and salt, they become soft and creamy with a slight crunch on the outside. These are guaranteed to become your new favourite roast potatoes.

SERVES 4

750g (1lb 10oz) white potatoes (about 4 large ones), quartered lengthways

4 tablespoons extra virgin olive oil

juice of 2 lemons

2 garlic cloves, grated

2 teaspoons dried oregano

salt to taste

1 Preheat the oven to 170°C fan (375°F), Gas Mark 5. Line a baking tray with baking paper.

2 Spread out the potatoes on the lined tray, add the other ingredients and season with salt to taste. Toss the potatoes in the dressing to coat well.

3 Roast the potatoes for 50 minutes, turning them halfway through, until they're soft and tender. Serve as part of a roast.

MOUSAKÁS

Moussaka

SERVES 6–8

2 large potatoes, very thinly sliced (about 1mm/ 1/16 inch)

2 aubergines, thinly sliced

4 tablespoons extra virgin olive oil

1 teaspoon fresh thyme leaves

salt and pepper

For the mince sauce

1–2 tablespoons extra virgin olive oil

1 red onion, chopped

1 tablespoon tomato purée

2 tablespoons dried oregano

½ teaspoon ground cinnamon, plus extra to finish

750g (1lb 10oz) minced beef (10% fat)

400g (14oz) can chopped tomatoes

1 vegetable stock cube, dissolved in 150ml (5fl oz) hot water

100ml (3½fl oz) red wine

2 bay leaves

For the béchamel

50g (1¾oz) butter

50g (1¾oz) plain flour

600ml (20fl oz) full-fat milk

pinch of ground cinnamon and grated nutmeg

70g (2½oz) Parmesan cheese, grated, to garnish

Moussaka is the classic Greek comfort meal... sliced roasted potato and aubergine layered with rich minced beef and topped with an even richer béchamel sauce. The wonderful thing about moussaka is that the flavours become even more pronounced as the dish cools down, making it perfect for leftovers (that's if you have any!). As with most of my recipes with a minced beef sauce, I'm using red wine, stock and a combination of seasonings to deepen its flavour. Despite the various cooking stages involved, my version requires minimal effort and creates little washing up; just whack the potato slices in the oven first then add the aubergine to the same tray while you get on with the sauces.

1 Preheat the oven to 180°C fan (400°F), Gas Mark 6. Spread the potato slices over a large, deep-sided baking tray (about 38 × 25cm/15 × 10 inches) and coat them in half the oil and half the thyme, and season with salt and pepper. Bake for 30 minutes.

2 Meanwhile, put the aubergine slices in a mixing bowl with the rest of the oil, thyme and seasoning. Stir to coat. Once the potatoes have softened (they don't need to be fully cooked through), remove the tray from the oven and evenly spread the aubergines over the potatoes. Return the tray to the oven for a further 30 minutes. After about 15 minutes, lower the temperature to 160°C fan (350°F), Gas Mark 4 so that the aubergines don't char too quickly.

3 Turn your attention to the mince sauce. Pour the oil into a saucepan and place over a medium heat. After 1–2 minutes stir in the onion. Cook for 2 minutes, until softened, then stir through the tomato purée, oregano and cinnamon, and season with salt and pepper.

4 Once the purée has darkened in colour, add the minced beef, breaking it up into chunks with the back of a wooden spoon to ensure it cooks evenly. Leave to brown fully for about 5 minutes.

»

5 Stir in the tomatoes, prepared vegetable stock, wine and bay leaves. Turn down the heat to low and cover the pan with a lid. Leave to simmer for 20–25 minutes, or until the sauce has reduced and the smell of the wine has dissipated.

6 Next, prepare the béchamel. Melt the butter in another large saucepan over a medium heat. Once it has melted, add the flour and whisk: it will form a thick roux. Slowly add the milk in 5–6 goes, whisking continuously to stop any clumps from forming, until the sauce thickens. Once thick, take the pan off the heat and whisk in a pinch of cinnamon and nutmeg.

7 Remove the tray of cooked aubergine and potatoes from the oven and turn up the temperature to 180°C fan (400°F), Gas Mark 6.

8 Layer the mince sauce over the aubergine and potato slices, spreading it out evenly. Then use a ladle to spread the béchamel to form a layer over the mince. Smooth carefully with a spatula to avoid blending the béchamel with the meat layer. Finally, top the béchamel with the grated Parmesan and a light dusting of cinnamon. Bake the assembled moussaka for 40 minutes until golden brown on top. Leave for an hour to cool at room temperature before slicing and serving – this ensures the layers remain intact.

TOP TIP You can use minced lamb instead of beef if you prefer – just make sure it's 10% fat. You can also substitute some or all of the aubergine for courgettes, cut lengthways into thin slices.

STIFÁDO

Slow-cooked Beef Stew

Stifado is the ultimate Greek comfort dish. It's a beef stew slow-cooked in a rich and aromatic tomato sauce, spiced with cinnamon, cloves and a touch of chilli flakes for heat, and caramelized shallots that provide a unique sweetness. I like to add red wine and beef stock to the sauce for depth of flavour, finishing it with a knob of butter for extra richness.

SERVES 4–6

- 3 tablespoons extra virgin olive oil
- 400g (14oz) shallots
- 700g (1lb 9oz) stewing beef, cut into chunks
- 50g (1¾oz) tomato purée
- 4 garlic cloves, crushed
- 400g (14oz) can chopped tomatoes
- 500ml (18fl oz) passata
- 1 tablespoon light brown sugar
- 2 tablespoons red wine
- 1 beef stock cube, crumbled
- 5 whole cloves
- 1 teaspoon ground cinnamon
- ¼ teaspoon chilli flakes
- 1 teaspoon dried oregano
- 2 bay leaves
- 30g (1oz) butter
- salt and pepper

1 Pour the oil into a large saucepan and place over a high heat. After a minute, add the shallots and cover the pan with a lid. Leave the shallots to soften and caramelize for 5 minutes, shaking the pan to turn them around or flipping them around using tongs (be careful with the hot oil), then reduce the heat to medium and cover the pan again. Once the shallots are golden brown, use a slotted spoon to transfer them to a bowl.

2 Add the beef chunks to the pan, in 2 batches if necessary so that the pan is not overcrowded. Brown the beef chunks for about 5 minutes, turning to colour on both sides.

3 Add the tomato purée and stir through to coat the beef. Then add the garlic, chopped tomatoes, passata, sugar, red wine, crumbled stock cube, spices, oregano and bay leaves. Season with a generous amount of salt and pepper, stir to combine then cover the pan with a lid and reduce the heat to low.

4 Simmer the *stifado* for a total of 3 hours, stirring occasionally throughout. The sauce will reduce, and the beef will become tender. After 2½ hours, add the caramelized shallots back into the pan and stir them through the sauce, along with the butter. Leave the stew to simmer, uncovered, for the final 30 minutes, to reduce the sauce even further.

5 When ready, remove the bay leaves and whole cloves. Serve the *stifado* with long-grain rice.

KLÉFTIKO

Slow-cooked Lamb

SERVES 4

1kg (2lb 4oz) white potatoes, diced

2 peppers (preferably 1 green and 1 red), stems and seeds removed, cut into 2.5cm (1 inch) dice

1 red onion, chopped

1.4kg (3lb) boneless shoulder of lamb

For the marinade

6 tablespoons extra virgin olive oil

8 teaspoons white wine vinegar

5 garlic cloves

1 teaspoon lemon zest

2 teaspoons dried oregano

½ teaspoon ground cinnamon

½ teaspoon ground pepper

1 teaspoon salt

For the lemon and honey glaze

juice of 1 lemon

1 tablespoon runny honey

If I had to pick one Greek dish to eat for the rest of my life, it would have to be *kléftiko*. Super-tender lamb coated in a garlicky, herby marinade and slow-cooked with lemony potatoes, peppers and red onions – what's not to love? The peppers and red onions become slightly charred when slow-cooked and add a subtle smokiness to the lamb. The trick to getting perfect juicy, tender meat is to seal in the moisture by double wrapping the roasting tray with baking paper and foil and tightly tucking in the sides. *Kléftiko* is the dish to make for a special occasion and it's surprisingly easy – just give it time to slow-cook to perfection!

1 Preheat the oven to 170°C fan (375°F), Gas Mark 5. Prepare a large roasting tray by lining it with foil.

2 Add the prepped veg to the roasting tray to form a layer. Remove the lamb shoulder from its packaging (remove any string as well), and place on top of the vegetables in the tray.

3 Make the marinade by putting all the ingredients in a food processor and blitzing for 1 minute. Pour the marinade over the meat and veg and, wearing disposable gloves, use your hands to fully coat everything.

4 Cover the tray with a sheet of baking paper, closing in the sides around the contents. Then wrap the top with a sheet of foil and seal in the sides tightly. Place the tray in the oven and cook for 4 hours.

5 Once the lamb has cooked, make the glaze by mixing together the lemon juice, honey and a little salt in a small bowl. Remove the foil and baking paper from the tray and drizzle the honey glaze over the lamb.

6 Return the tray to the oven and cook for another 20–30 minutes or until the top of the lamb is crispy.

7 Before plating up, I like to shred the lamb so that it absorbs all the delicious juices in the tray. Serve the *kléftiko* warm.

MELITZANÓPITA STRIFTÍ

Aubergine Filo Pie

Melitzanópita is a rich savoury pie with a roasted aubergine and feta cheese filling stuffed in layers of buttery filo pastry and assembled to form a spiral shape. It's delicate from the tender aubergine and perfectly balanced by the sweetness of the roasted red pepper. It can be served as an appetizer or enjoyed as a meal on its own.

SERVES 4

9 filo pastry sheets

olive oil, for brushing

1 heaped teaspoon black sesame seeds

For the filling

2 aubergines, trimmed and halved lengthways

2 pointed red peppers, halved lengthways, stems and seeds removed

3 tablespoons extra virgin olive oil

1 white onion, chopped

3 garlic cloves, crushed

4 spring onions, finely chopped

50g (1¾oz) parsley, finely chopped

20g (¾oz) mint leaves, finely chopped

200g (7oz) feta cheese, crumbled

1 egg

salt and pepper

1 Preheat the oven to 180°C fan (400°F), Gas Mark 6 and line a baking tray with baking paper.

2 Score the cut side of the aubergines and place them and the halved peppers on the lined baking tray. Drizzle with half the olive oil and season with salt. Rub the vegetables to coat them evenly in oil and salt, and bake for 30 minutes or until softened.

3 Pour the remaining oil into a frying pan and place over a low heat. After 2 minutes, add the onion and cook for 5 minutes until softened. Then add the crushed garlic and cook for a further minute, stirring frequently. Take the pan off the heat and set aside.

4 Once the aubergines and red peppers are cooked, place them in a bowl and cover it with clingfilm to trap the moisture and make it easier to peel off the skin from the peppers. Leave them to cool for 15 minutes before scooping the flesh from the aubergines and peeling off the pepper skin. Keep the lined tray – you will need it later. Meanwhile preheat the oven to 180°C fan (400°F), Gas Mark 6.

5 Roughly mash the vegetables on a chopping board and return them to the same bowl, along with the cooked onion and remaining ingredients. Season generously with salt and pepper and mix everything until fully combined.

6 Use the same lined tray to bake the *melitzanópita*. Layer up 3 sheets of filo pastry and brush some oil on top. Place a third of the mixture at the bottom of the first sheet and carefully roll from the bottom up to form a log shape. Once the sheet is fully rolled, starting from one end of the log, roll it inwards towards the other end to form a spiral shape. Place on the lined baking tray.

7 Use the remaining 6 sheets of filo to create 2 more filo logs, this time wrapping them around the first spiral shape to create one large pie. Brush the top with more olive oil and sprinkle with the sesame seeds.

8 Bake the *melitzanópita* for 30 minutes or until golden on top. Allow to cool for 10 minutes before serving.

Share

Like a Greek

6. Shar

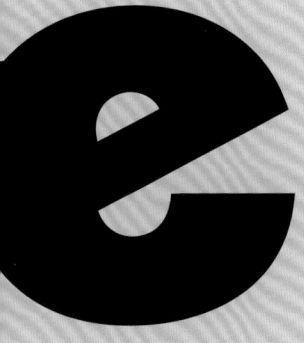

Consider this chapter your one-stop shop for a variety of Greek sweet and savoury treats that are best enjoyed when shared. During festive celebrations, it's traditional to make, for example, **koulourákia** (Easter cookies) or **kourabiedés** (buttery shortbread, usually made over Christmas) in large batches so that they can be given to loved ones as tokens of appreciation. Other goodies include: **spiral-shaped filo pastries**, chewy **pastéli** – a two-ingredient power bar made from sesame seeds and honey; **amygdalotá** – the most incredible almond meringue cookies; and **paximádia** – Greek-style biscotti that are twice-baked and perfect for dunking into a cuppa.

TYRÓPSOMO

Greek Cheese Bread

Infused with crushed coriander seeds for a mildly floral taste, and stuffed with crumbled feta and fresh mint, these beautifully soft, cheesy bread rolls are the perfect snack or accompaniment to a meal. I love to serve *tyrópsomo* with my *revythiá* (see page 103), or share them with friends I've invited round for dinner. The rolls are simple to make and such a treat when you're craving something savoury and heartwarming.

MAKES 10

360ml (12½fl oz) lukewarm water

1 tablespoon sugar

10g (¼oz) active dry yeast

600g (1lb 5oz) white bread flour, plus extra for dusting

1 tablespoon extra virgin olive oil

2 tablespoons coriander seeds, crushed

pinch of salt

200g (7oz) feta cheese, crumbled

30g (1oz) mint leaves, finely chopped

1 Add the lukewarm water and sugar to a large mixing bowl and whisk until combined. Then stir in the active dry yeast and leave to stand for 2 minutes until frothy on top. Sift in the flour and mix it into the wet ingredients using a spoon to form a rough dough.

2 Knead the dough by hand for 8 minutes or transfer to a stand mixer fitted with a dough hook and knead for 4 minutes. Halfway through kneading, add the oil, coriander seeds and salt.

3 Return the dough to the mixing bowl and cover with a clean tea towel. Leave at room temperature to prove for 1½ hours or until risen and doubled in size.

4 Once the dough has risen, preheat the oven to 180°C fan (400°F), Gas Mark 6 and line a baking tray with baking paper. Lightly flour the work surface and roll out the dough to a rectangle roughly 50 × 30cm (20 × 12 inches).

5 Sprinkle the feta and mint evenly over the dough. Then carefully roll up the dough lengthways to form a log shape. Cut this into 10 even pieces.

6 Place the rolls, spaced apart, on the lined tray and leave to rise, uncovered, for another 10 minutes.

7 Bake for 32–35 minutes or until the rolls are lightly brown on top. Transfer to a wire rack and serve warm. The rolls will last for 2 days in an airtight container and are best reheated before serving.

ELAIOPITÁKIA AND HALLOUMOPITÁKIA

Olive Bread and Halloumi Bread

MAKES 8

300ml (10fl oz) lukewarm water

1 teaspoon runny honey

7g (1 sachet) fast-action dried yeast

500g (1lb 2oz) plain flour, plus extra for dusting

pinch of salt

For the olive filling

3 spring onions, finely chopped

50g (1¾oz) fresh coriander, chopped

120g (4oz) Kalamata olives, pitted and finely chopped

olive oil, for drizzling

OR

For the halloumi filling

5 spring onions, finely chopped

50g (1¾oz) fresh coriander, chopped

150–200g (5½–7oz) halloumi, chopped

olive oil, for drizzling

Elaiopitákia and *halloumopitákia* are an ode to my Greek-Cypriot heritage. Commonly found in Cypriot bakeries and known as *almýra*, which means savoury in Greek, these are pastry or bread rolls stuffed with chopped olives or halloumi, with spring onions, fresh coriander and a healthy drizzle of extra virgin olive oil. Growing up, I used to come home to the smell of a freshly baked batch made by my *yiayiá* (grandma). Here I'm giving you both filling options to try.

1 Add the lukewarm water and teaspoon of honey to a large mixing bowl and whisk until combined. Then stir in the dried yeast and leave to stand for 2 minutes until frothy on top. Sift in the flour and mix it into the wet ingredients using a spoon to form a rough dough.

2 Knead the dough by hand for 8 minutes or transfer to a stand mixer fitted with a dough hook and knead for 4 minutes. Halfway through kneading, add the pinch of salt.

3 Return the dough to the mixing bowl, sprinkle some flour on top and cover with a clean tea towel. Leave to prove at room temperature for at least 1 hour until it has risen and doubled in size.

4 Preheat the oven to 170°C fan (375°F), Gas Mark 5 and line a baking tray with baking paper. Mix together the ingredients (except the oil) for your chosen filling.

5 Once risen, put the dough on a lightly floured surface. Divide into 8 equal portions and form into balls. Roll each dough ball using a rolling pin, adding extra flour if necessary, until it stretches to roughly the size of a small side plate.

6 Place a tablespoon of your chosen filling into the middle of the first dough piece. Drizzle some oil on top and carefully roll up the dough to form a log and stretch and twist it from both ends to hold the filling. Roll from one end to form a spiral shape. Repeat with the remaining dough and filling.

7 Place the rolls, spaced apart, on the lined tray and leave to rise, uncovered, for 15 minutes.

8 Bake for 25–30 minutes until lightly golden and the bread sounds hollow when you tap the bottom of the roll. Remove the tray from the oven and allow the rolls to cool for 10 minutes before serving. Enjoy them warm. They keep for up to 3 days in an airtight container and are best reheated.

ALEVRÓPITA

Thin-battered Cheese Pie

I like to think of *alevrópita* as the Greek version of a British Yorkshire pudding: light and spongy in texture, with a copious amount of crumbled feta. Greeks refer to savoury baked goods like this as *almýra*, and these do well as a mid-afternoon snack, especially if you have guests round for tea. This thin feta pie comes together with a handful of ingredients that are whisked to form a batter. Feta is then crumbled and swirled on top, which becomes beautifully golden brown once baked.

MAKES 12

3 tablespoons extra virgin olive oil
200g (7oz) plain flour
200ml (7fl oz) full-fat milk
2 large eggs
100ml (3½fl oz) water
200g (7oz) feta cheese
salt to taste

1 Preheat the oven to 200°C fan (425°F), Gas Mark 7 and grease a nonstick traybake tin (I used a 25 × 32cm/10 × 12½ inch tin) with 1 tablespoon of the oil – this makes the *alevrópita* crispy at the base.

2 To make the batter, add the flour, milk and eggs to a mixing bowl and whisk until they homogenize. The consistency will be thick at this stage. Add the measured water and salt and whisk again to combine.

3 Pour in the remaining oil and roughly crumble the feta into the batter. Using a spatula, gently swirl the batter, without overmixing – you want some of the oil to sit on top of the batter to give the pie a crispy top.

4 Pour the batter into the tray and bake for 35–40 minutes until it's golden and crispy on top.

5 Once it's baked, carefully flip the *alevrópita* on to a chopping board and slice it into 12 pieces. Enjoy it as a snack, preferably warm. Stored in an airtight container it will keep for 2 days.

SPANAKÓPITES STRIFTÉS

Spinach Pie Filo Swirls

I'm betting you already love the all-time classic, *spanakópita*, so let me introduce you to what is set to become your new favourite way to enjoy this pie! Layers of filo, rolled to form a log and then shaped into mini pies, become even more crispy and delicious cooked this way. What's more, you can easily transport *spanakópites striftés* to gatherings or enjoy them on the go – no need to slice and serve. If you're using filo pastry bought from a Greek or Turkish shop, I recommend using three sheets per pie as this type of filo tends to be thinner; if using filo from a regular supermarket, two slices should suffice.

MAKES 6

For the filling

400g (14oz) baby spinach, washed and drained

2 tablespoons extra virgin olive oil

1 leek, finely chopped

1 teaspoon ground cinnamon

¼ teaspoon grated nutmeg

¼ teaspoon ground black pepper

50g (1¾oz) dill fronds, chopped

200g (7oz) feta cheese, crumbled

salt to taste

For the pie

12–18 filo pastry sheets (depending on brand)

8 teaspoons extra virgin olive oil

black sesame seeds

1 Start with the filling. Place a large saucepan over a medium heat. After a minute, add a few handfuls of the spinach and cover the saucepan with a lid. The spinach will begin to wilt after 30 seconds or so, at which point remove the lid and stir the spinach. After about another minute, it will wilt even more and darken in colour. Remove from the pan and place in a sieve over a bowl and repeat this process with the rest of the spinach. Set aside and let it cool.

2 Put the pan back over a medium heat and add the oil and leek. Cook for around 2–3 minutes until it softens, then add the spices and cook for a further 2 minutes, stirring regularly throughout. At this point, stir through the dill, feta and cooked spinach. Remove the pan from the heat.

3 Preheat the oven to 180°C fan (400°F), Gas Mark 6 and line a large baking tray with baking paper.

4 To assemble the pies, layer 2 sheets of pastry, one on top of the other, and brush the top 3 or 4 times with extra virgin olive oil, brushing the entire surface evenly. Roughly a quarter of the way up from the bottom of the sheets, place 4–5 tablespoons of the spinach filling in a row, leaving space between each one. Use a spatula to spread out the spoonfuls to form a line of filling across the sheet. Working from the bottom up, tightly roll the filo sheets over the filling to form a log. Next, starting at one end of the log, gently roll it inwards to form a spiral shape. Use the spatula to carefully transfer the pie on to the lined tray. Repeat this process with the remaining filo sheets and filling to make 6 spirals.

5 Once all the pastries have been filled, rolled and shaped, brush the tops with extra virgin olive oil and sprinkle with a pinch of sesame seeds. Bake for a total of 40 minutes, reducing the temperature to 150°C fan (345°F), Gas Mark 3½ after 20 minutes.

6 Once baked, leave the *spanakópites striftés* to cool for 10 minutes before serving. *Spanakópites* are best enjoyed warm and you can reheat them the next day.

KYPRIAKÁ BOURÉKIA ME ANARÍ

Cypriot Sweet Cheese Dumplings

MAKES 12

300ml (10fl oz) sunflower oil, for frying

10–15g (¼–½oz) icing sugar

½ teaspoon ground cinnamon

For the pastry

250g (9oz) plain flour, plus extra for dusting

2 tablespoons vegetable oil

115ml (4fl oz) water

½ teaspoon white wine vinegar

¼ teaspoon salt

For the filling

250g (9oz) fresh anari cheese (or ricotta)

50g (1¾oz) caster sugar

1 teaspoon ground cinnamon

1 tablespoon rose water

These crispy crescent-shaped dumplings, known as *bourékia* in Greek, are a sweet treat worthy of any occasion. They are made with thin pastry filled with anari cheese, a soft and mild cheese from Cyprus that is similar to ricotta (which makes a good substitute if you can't find anari), mixed with a hint of rose water for a lightly floral taste and then shallow-fried until crisp and golden. The trick to achieving perfectly crispy pastry is to add a hint of vinegar to the dough. To finish, the *bourékia* are then lightly dusted in icing sugar and cinnamon. Irresistible!

1 First make the pastry. Put all the ingredients except the salt in a large mixing bowl and stir to homogenize. Once a dough forms, transfer it either to a stand mixer fitted with a dough hook or, if working by hand, to a work surface lightly dusted with flour. Knead the dough for 5 minutes if using a stand mixer or for 10 minutes if working by hand, adding the salt halfway through the kneading. Once the dough is firm, return it to the mixing bowl, cover and refrigerate for 30 minutes.

2 Meanwhile, prepare the filling by combining all the ingredients in a large mixing bowl. I like to mash up the anari with a fork then mix through the sugar, cinnamon and rose water to a paste-like texture.

3 Once the dough has chilled, place it on a lightly floured work surface and roll it out as thinly as possible without tearing it, aiming for a thickness of 2–3mm (¹⁄₁₆ inch). Use a small bowl or a large cookie cutter (about 13cm/5 inches in diameter) to cut out discs, gathering all the trimmings, kneading and re-rolling to get as many as possible.

>>

4 Place a heaped tablespoon of the filling in the middle of each disc and fold the pastry in half to form a crescent shape. Use a fork to seal the edges and create a nice pattern for the *bourékia*. Transfer your assembled *bourékia* to a large plate and line a second plate with kitchen paper.

5 Pour the sunflower oil into a large frying pan and place over a high heat. After 2–3 minutes, to test it's hot enough, stick the tip of a wooden spoon into the pan to see if the oil bubbles up around it. Carefully drop the *bourékia* in one at a time, leaving space between them. I recommend frying the *bourékia* in batches, so as not to overcrowd the pan. Fry for 3–4 minutes, flipping them halfway through, until crispy and golden brown.

6 Transfer the fried *bourékia* to the lined plate to drain off any excess oil and continue to fry the rest.

7 To serve, dust the *bourékia* in icing sugar and ground cinnamon before enjoying them warm.

AIR FRYER You can reheat *bourékia* in an air fryer at 180°C (350°F) for 3 minutes.

FLAOÚNES

Cypriot Cheese Pies

These savoury-sweet cheese pies are a traditional Easter treat for Greek-Cypriots. The spongy cheese filling is made using a Cypriot hard cheese called Flaoúna combined with raisins and fresh mint, and the shortcrust pastry includes ground mastic and mahlepi, spices that give it a distinctive aroma. If you cannot find Flaoúna, use a 50:50 combination of halloumi and Cheddar cheese, and if you cannot source mastic and mahlepi, try ground aniseed and ground cardamom.

MAKES 26

For the filling

1.2kg (2lb 11oz) Flaoúna cheese, grated
60g (2¼oz) mint leaves, chopped
200g (7oz) raisins
10 large eggs
150g (5½oz) self-raising flour
1 teaspoon baking powder
1 teaspoon ground mastic
1 teaspoon ground mahlepi

For the dough

600ml (20fl oz) lukewarm water
20g (¾oz) active dry yeast
100g (3½oz) caster sugar
1kg (2lb 4oz) plain flour, plus extra for dusting
1 teaspoon ground mastic
1 teaspoon ground mahlepi
sesame seeds, for sprinkling
2 eggs, beaten, for brushing

1 To make the filling, put the Flaoúna in a very large mixing bowl, add the rest of the ingredients and mix to combine – the consistency will be spongy. Set aside.

2 For the dough, pour the lukewarm water into another bowl. Add the sugar and yeast and whisk until frothy. Leave to settle for 2 minutes. Sift the flour over the liquid mixture and stir with a wooden spoon to combine the ingredients and form a dough. Transfer it either to a stand mixer fitted with a dough hook or, if working by hand, to a work surface lightly dusted with flour. Knead the dough for 4 minutes if using a stand mixer or for 8 minutes if working by hand, adding the ground mastic and mahlepi halfway through the kneading.

3 Once kneaded, lightly dust the dough with flour. Cover with a clean tea towel and leave to prove at room temperature for 1 hour or until risen and doubled in size.

4 Preheat the oven to 180°C fan (400°F), Gas Mark 6 and line 2 large baking trays with baking paper. Divide the dough evenly into 26 balls. Lightly flour a rolling pin and roll out the first ball into a circle and sprinkle with sesame seeds. Carefully flip the flattened dough and add 2–3 tablespoons of the cheese mixture in the centre. Fold the dough in from three sides to form a triangle shape, leaving the middle bit uncovered to reveal the filling. Repeat with the rest of the mixture and dough.

5 Place the prepared *flaoúnes* on the lined baking trays and brush the tops with egg wash. Bake for 25–30 minutes until beautifully golden brown. Leave to cool on a wire rack for at least 10 minutes.

6 Store in an airtight container and eat within 5 days. *Flaoúnes* are best enjoyed warm, so reheat them in a low oven.

KOULOURÁKIA

Greek Easter Cookies

These biscuits are typically enjoyed after Holy Saturday in the Greek Orthodox tradition. Delicately crispy on the outside and soft and buttery within, they're flavoured with orange zest as well as mahlepi (if you can get your hands on this spice; if not, ground cardamom is a good alternative) for a unique aroma. It only takes a few staple ingredients to make *koulourákia* and with this recipe you don't need to chill the dough before shaping it. Fun fact: the braiding of the cookie dough – the traditional way to shape *koulourákia* – symbolizes the intertwining of faith and family. But you can shape yours however you like: into a spiral, an s-shape or even like a pretzel.

MAKES 20

150g (5½oz) butter, at room temperature

130g (4½oz) caster sugar

zest of ½ orange

8 teaspoons orange juice

1 large egg, plus 1 egg yolk, beaten, for brushing

450g (1lb) plain flour

½ teaspoon baking powder

¼ teaspoon bicarbonate of soda

1 teaspoon ground mahlepi

1 Preheat the oven to 180°C fan (400°F), Gas Mark 6 and line a baking tray with baking paper.

2 Put the butter and sugar in the bowl of a stand mixer and beat on a high speed for 5 minutes until light and fluffy. Add the orange zest and juice and the whole egg. Continue to beat for a further 2 minutes.

3 Meanwhile, in a separate bowl, sift the flour, baking powder, bicarbonate of soda and mahlepi, and stir through with a spoon to roughly combine. Add the dry ingredients to the wet ingredients in 2 goes, beating on a high speed until the mixture homogenizes. The consistency will be firm and malleable.

4 Transfer the dough to a work surface. Taking about a tablespoonful of the dough, weighing about 40g (1½oz), using your hands, roll the piece to form a thin strip. Fold in the strip so that the 2 ends are touching and twist the strip to form a braid shape. Repeat this process with the rest of the dough and place them on the lined tray spaced apart.

5 Brush egg yolk over the tops of the cookies and bake for 18 minutes until they're lightly golden.

6 Transfer to a wire rack and leave to cool for 15 minutes. Enjoy the *koulourákia* with a hot drink and you can store them in an airtight container for up to a week.

PASTÉLI

Honey Sesame Bars

Often referred to as the ancient version of a power bar, this two-ingredient confection is the perfect snack for when you're craving something sweet. I recommend using a good-quality honey – like a strong dark one from Greece, which is naturally bold and more floral in flavour. My recipe makes a perfectly chewy version that's totally moreish and very simple to make – the hardest part is waiting for them to cool down. *Pastéli* last for a good week (that's if you don't indulge in them all in one go!).

MAKES 16

250g (9oz) white sesame seeds

250ml (9fl oz) good-quality runny honey

1 Line a 23cm (9 inch) square baking dish or tray with baking paper.

2 Put the sesame seeds in a frying pan over a medium heat. Toast them for 10–12 minutes until they turn a light golden colour, continuously stirring the pan to prevent the seeds from burning.

3 Tip the toasted sesame seeds on to a plate. Place the pan over a high heat and add the honey. Once it starts to bubble and foam, return the sesame seeds to the pan. Stir continuously for 5 minutes.

4 Pour the *pastéli* into the lined dish and use the back of a spoon to press the mixture into an even layer.

5 Leave to cool for 20 minutes before cutting into bars.

PAXIMÁDIA

Greek-style Biscotti

These biscotti are a crunchy treat – and perfect for dunking into a cuppa. There is also a savoury version, made with wholewheat or barley flour, but this recipe for sweet and aromatic *paximádia* includes orange zest and juice, cinnamon and mahlepi (a spice derived from cherry kernels, which is optional). The *paximádia* are covered in sesame seeds before being twice baked and left to cool to become fully crunchy. What's amazing is that they come together in just one bowl! Bake them for your friends and they're sure to be a crowd-pleaser.

MAKES 16–18

300g (10½oz) plain flour

150g (5½oz) caster sugar

1 teaspoon ground cinnamon

½ teaspoon ground mahlepi (optional)

1 teaspoon baking powder

5 tablespoons extra virgin olive oil

zest and juice of 1 orange (you need 100ml/3½fl oz)

50g (1¾oz) almonds, chopped

pinch of salt

To decorate

2 tablespoons white sesame seeds

1 tablespoon black sesame seeds

1 Preheat the oven to 170°C fan (375°F), Gas Mark 5 and line a large baking tray with baking paper. Put the white and black sesame seeds in a small bowl, stir to combine then set aside.

2 Add all the ingredients to a large bowl and, using your hands or a wooden spoon, mix to combine everything and form a dough.

3 Turn out the dough on to a board and shape into a ball. Cut it in half and, using your hands, roll each one into a log shape roughly 30cm (12 inches) long and 5–7cm (2–3 inches) in diameter.

4 Cover the tops of both logs in sesame seeds (a quick roll on the board will help to press them in). Carefully turn over the logs and repeat with the remaining seeds.

5 Place the seed-coated logs on the lined baking tray and make light diagonal incisions to mark roughly 8 or 9 slices on each one. Then bake for 30 minutes.

6 Remove the tray from the oven and transfer the logs to a wire rack to cool for 10 minutes. Using a serrated knife, carefully slice through the incision marks and spread out the slices on the tray. Increase the temperature to 200°C fan (425°F), Gas Mark 7 and bake the *paximádia* a second time for a further 12 minutes. Switch off the heat and leave the biscuits in the oven for a final 5 minutes then place them on a wire rack to cool completely and become crunchy.

7 Enjoy with your preferred cuppa. Store them in an airtight container and eat within 3 days.

GLYKÉS KOLOKYTHÓPITES STRIFTÉS

Filo Pumpkin Pies

MAKES 6

100g (3½oz) butter, melted
12 filo pastry sheets
1 tablespoon icing sugar, to decorate

For the syrup

100g (3½oz) caster sugar
100ml (3½fl oz) water
½ cinnamon stick
2 strips of orange peel

For the filling

150g (5½oz) walnuts
425g (15oz) can pumpkin purée
100g (3½oz) raisins
100g (3½oz) caster sugar
1 teaspoon vanilla extract
1½ teaspoons ground cinnamon
½ teaspoon ground ginger
½ teaspoon grated nutmeg
¼ teaspoon ground cloves

Delightfully crispy on the outside and deliciously aromatic within, these pumpkin pies use pumpkin purée instead of fresh pumpkin, so they are really simple to whip up. Once baked, each pastry is soaked in a delicious orange-flavoured syrup.

1 Add all the ingredients for the syrup to a saucepan and place over a high heat. Using a spatula, gently stir while the sugar dissolves and, once the syrup comes to the boil, immediately take the pan off the heat and set aside to cool.

2 Next, prepare the filling. Tip the walnuts into a food processor and blitz them for 15–20 seconds, or until they are crushed. Add them to a large mixing bowl along with the remaining ingredients and mix everything until well combined.

3 Before assembling the pumpkin pies, preheat the oven to 180°C fan (400°F), Gas Mark 6 and line a large baking tray with baking paper. Have your melted butter ready and unwrap the filo pastry.

4 Layer 2 sheets of pastry, one on top of the other, and use a brush to dot some melted butter on the top sheet in four or five different spots. Brush this over the entire surface, spreading it evenly. About a quarter of the way up from the bottom of the sheets, add 4–5 tablespoons of the pumpkin filling in a row, leaving space between each one. Use a spatula to spread out the spoonfuls to form a line of filling across the sheet. Working from the bottom up, tightly roll the filo sheets over the filling to form a log. Next, starting at one end of the log, gently roll it inwards to form a spiral shape. Use the spatula to carefully transfer the pie on to the lined tray. Repeat this process with the remaining filo sheets and pumpkin filling to make 6 spirals.

5 Once all the pastries have been filled, rolled and shaped, brush the tops with more melted butter (you may not need all of it). Bake for 45 minutes until the pies are crispy and golden on top.

6 Remove the tray from the oven and spoon 2–3 tablespoons of the syrup over the pies while they are still hot. Allow them to absorb the syrup for 10 minutes. Lightly dust the tops with icing sugar and serve the *kolokythópites* warm.

TACHINÓPITES

Cypriot Tahini Pies

These incredible sweet tahini pastries are popular in Cyprus during Lent. They contain a dreamy filling with a unique flavour profile: think of them as an elaborate cinnamon bun – jammy and caramelized in texture from the melted tahini, and distinctly aromatic thanks to the cinnamon and carob syrup, a natural sweetener that tastes similar to dates. The dough is stuffed with the filling, twisted and rolled to form cute spirals. Once baked, they're glazed with melted honey and are just simply divine.

MAKES 8

300ml (10fl oz) lukewarm water

1 teaspoon runny honey, plus extra, melted, for glazing

7g (1 sachet) fast-action dried yeast

500g (1lb 2oz) plain flour, plus extra for dusting

pinch of salt

For the filling

120g (4oz) tahini

100g (3½oz) caster sugar

2 tablespoons carob syrup

1 teaspoon ground cinnamon

1 Pour the lukewarm water into a large mixing bowl and add the teaspoon of honey, then whisk until combined. Stir in the dried yeast and leave to stand for 2 minutes until frothy on top. Sift in the flour and mix it into the wet ingredients using a spoon to form a rough dough.

2 Knead the dough by hand for 8 minutes or transfer to a stand mixer fitted with a dough hook and knead for 4 minutes. Halfway through kneading, add the salt. Return the dough to the mixing bowl, sprinkle some flour on top and cover with a clean tea towel. Leave to rise for at least 1 hour until it doubles in size.

3 Meanwhile, prepare the filling by combining the ingredients in a bowl. Mix thoroughly using a spatula until a thick paste forms. Preheat the oven to 170°C fan (375°F), Gas Mark 5 and line a baking tray with baking paper.

4 Once the dough has risen, transfer it to a lightly floured surface and divide into 8 equal portions, and roll into balls. One at a time, flatten each ball using the palm of your hand and place a heaped tablespoon of the filling in the middle. Then carefully roll up the dough to form a log and stretch and twist it from both ends to hold the filling. Roll from one end to form a spiral shape.

5 Place the pastries on the lined tray and bake for 23 minutes until lightly golden on top.

6 Remove the tray from the oven and lightly glaze the pies with melted honey. Enjoy them warm. They will keep for 3 days in an airtight container and are best reheated for maximum flavour.

AMYGDALOTÁ

Greek Almond Cookies

Slightly crispy on the outside and deliciously chewy in the middle, these traditional Cypriot almond meringue cookies, also known as *pastítsia* or Greek macaroons, are very popular at Greek weddings. Made with just a handful of ingredients, they come together in less than 30 minutes and are a delight. I love using both ground almonds and almond extract in the dough for extra flavour. The great thing about *amygdalotá* is that you can shape them however you like – rounds, swirls or crescents – I opt for fuss-free round shapes. There's no need for a perfect finish either because the rougher the edges, the crispier they become.

MAKES 16
3 large egg whites
300g (10½oz) ground almonds
300g (10½oz) icing sugar
1 teaspoon almond extract
handful of almond flakes

1 Preheat the oven to 170°C fan (375°F), Gas Mark 5 and line a baking tray with baking paper. Using a stand mixer, or handheld electric whisk and a bowl, whisk the egg whites on high speed to form soft peaks.

2 Sift the icing sugar into another mixing bowl, add the ground almonds and stir to combine then tip them into the bowl of whipped egg whites. Add the almond extract and mix well using a spatula until you have a sticky but malleable mixture.

3 Working with 2 tablespoons, scoop up a heaped tablespoon of the mixture and pass it between the 2 tablespoons to form a round shape. Place this on the lined paper. Repeat with the rest of the dough, spacing the cookies apart on the tray.

4 Place a couple of almond flakes on each cookie and bake for 15 minutes until lightly golden and slightly crispy on the edges.

5 Carefully transfer the *amygdalotá* to a wire rack and leave to cool for 15 minutes before enjoying or store in an airtight container and they will keep for up to 5 days. They also make the perfect little gift for a friend.

MOSAÏKÓ

Chocolate Salami

Mosaïkó, or *kormos* as it's also known in Greece, is a no-bake chocolate 'salami' – a slice of this is the perfect little sweet treat. It gets its name from the mosaic-like pattern created by the crushed biscuits that are coated in a decadent chocolate mixture infused with brandy and orange zest. Slice it up just like salami and enjoy with coffee or take with you when you're on the go.

MAKES 10–12

300g (10½oz) petit beurre biscuits

397g (14oz) can condensed milk

200g (7oz) plain dark chocolate, melted

100g (3½oz) butter, melted

3 tablespoons cocoa powder

1 teaspoon brandy

zest of 1 orange

1 Put the biscuits in a large bowl and very roughly break them up with your hands into little chunks (don't break them up too much as you want there to be a mosaic pattern in the salami). Set aside.

2 In another large mixing bowl, use a spatula to gently mix together the condensed milk, melted chocolate and melted butter until silky smooth. Add the remaining ingredients and mix again until combined.

3 Add the broken biscuits to the chocolate mixture and gently mix everything together until the biscuits are evenly coated.

4 Line a 450g (1lb) loaf tin with a large sheet of clingfilm, ensuring it overhangs the tin on all sides. Carefully pour in the biscuit mixture in several goes, pressing and flattening each addition into the tin using a spatula. Press and flatten the top and cover with the overhanging clingfilm.

5 Place the tin in the freezer for 2 hours to harden the salami. Then turn the salami out of the tin, unwrap and cut into slices. This will keep for 1 week in an airtight container in the fridge.

MOSAÏKÓ LEFKIS SOKOLÁTAS

White Chocolate Salami

This version of *mosaïkó* uses white chocolate, dried cranberries and extra brandy for that boozy kick. The flavour combination is heavenly and every bite will remind you of the festive season. That said, it's so delicious and simple to make, there's no reason why it can't be made all year round.

MAKES 10–12

300g (10½oz) petit beurre biscuits

397g (14oz) can condensed milk

200g white chocolate, melted

100g (3½oz) butter, melted

2 teaspoons brandy

50g (1¾oz) dried cranberries

zest of 1 orange

1 Put the biscuits in a large bowl and very roughly break them up with your hands into little chunks (don't break them up too much as you want there to be a mosaic pattern in the salami). Set aside.

2 In another large mixing bowl, use a spatula to gently mix together the condensed milk, melted chocolate and melted butter until silky smooth. Add the remaining ingredients and mix again until combined.

3 Add the broken biscuits to the chocolate mixture and gently mix everything together until the biscuits are evenly coated.

4 Line a 450g (1lb) loaf tin with a large sheet of clingfilm, ensuring it overhangs the tin on all sides. Carefully pour in the biscuit mixture in several goes, pressing and flattening each addition into the tin using a spatula. Press and flatten the top and cover with the overhanging clingfilm.

5 Place the tin in the freezer for 2 hours to harden the salami. Then turn the salami out of the tin, unwrap and cut into slices. This will keep for 1 week in an airtight container in the fridge.

KOURABIEDÉS

Greek Festive Shortbread

These buttery almond biscuits are like snowballs of joy – completely blanketed in icing sugar – and are the perfect treat over Christmas. Every Greek family has its own version, and I want to give a special shout out to my mum for teaching me her recipe: she insists on using corn oil, which helps to create the delicate but crumbly texture. Made with blanched almonds, *kourabiedés* are crunchy on the outside with a melt-in-the-mouth middle. You can infuse them with different flavourings, like orange or lemon zest, but the traditional way is to add brandy. The baked *kourabiedés* will be crumbly at first, but once cooled, they become irresistibly buttery. Unless you devour them in one go they will last for several weeks.

MAKES 30

300ml (10fl oz) corn oil

150g (5½oz) butter, melted

1 tablespoon brandy (2 tablespoons if you like things boozy!)

1 teaspoon vanilla extract

100g (3½oz) icing sugar, sifted, plus extra for dredging

1 egg yolk

100g (3½oz) blanched almonds, chopped

900g (2lb) plain flour

1 Preheat the oven to 150°C fan (345°F), Gas Mark 3½ and line a large baking tray with baking paper. Select a very large mixing bowl and add the oil, butter, brandy, vanilla extract, icing sugar and egg yolk. Mix together until everything is well combined.

2 Add the almonds and flour to the wet ingredients and mix to incorporate – the consistency will be crumbly but that's to be expected.

3 Take a heaped tablespoonful of the mixture and use your hands to roll it into a ball, or form into an oval, star or crescent shape if you wish. Continue with the rest of the mixture to make about 30 biscuits.

4 Place the biscuits on the lined tray, spaced apart, and bake for 20 minutes, or until lightly golden on top.

5 Once baked, allow the *kourabiedés* to cool on a wire rack for 10–15 minutes. Then transfer them on to a tray and dredge them in icing sugar until they're fully covered.

6 Stored in an airtight container, *kourabiedés* will keep for up to 3 weeks.

Sweet Lik

Treats

e a

Greek

7. Sweet Treats

ts

These recipes will fill those moments in the day when all you want is to satisfy your sweet cravings. Here are fuss-free treats, custard-filled desserts, nutty concoctions and more. I've included the very best syrup-soaked cakes, known as **siropiastá** in Greek, from the juiciest **lemonópita** (lemon filo cake) to lesser-known ones like **indokaridópita** (coconut cake) that deserve equal attention. Beyond this syrupy goodness are simple yet decadent dairy-based treats, such as Greek-inspired yogurt-based **cheesecake** with a gingernut base, or **balsamic-roasted strawberries** served on a bed of yogurt. As so often in this book, I've reimagined the classics – giving creamy **rice pudding** an aromatic twist, and swirling raspberries into my lemon filo cake. There are plant-based desserts here too – try my no-bake Greek-style **halva** (a semolina-based pudding) or **ladópita**, a rich and zesty cake made using extra virgin olive oil and orange juice.

LADÓPITA

Olive Oil Cake

Delightfully crispy on the outside with a moreish tender crumb, *ladópita*, also known as *fanourópita*, is a showstopper of a cake. The cake gets its name from the Greek word *elaiólado*, which means 'olive oil', a nod to the *ladópita*'s use of olive oil instead of eggs in the batter. Here, I use extra virgin olive oil for richness and orange juice for aroma, plus ground cinnamon and cloves for spice. It requires very little effort: simply prepare the wet ingredients before whisking in the dry. There's no need to let this cake chill, as it's best enjoyed warm.

SERVES 15

180g (6¼oz) caster sugar

180ml (6fl oz) extra virgin olive oil, plus extra for greasing

zest of 2 oranges

225ml (8fl oz) fresh orange juice

320g (11½oz) plain flour

2 tsp baking powder

½ teaspoon bicarbonate of soda

1½ teaspoons ground cinnamon

¼ teaspoon ground cloves

2 tablespoons sesame seeds, to decorate

1. Preheat the oven to 170°C fan (375°F), Gas Mark 5. Grease a nonstick 32 × 22cm (12½ × 8½ inch) traybake tin with olive oil.

2. Whisk together the sugar and oil in a large bowl until combined. Add the orange zest and juice and whisk again. Into a separate bowl, sift the flour, baking powder, bicarbonate of soda and spices, stirring to combine.

3. Add the dry ingredients to the wet in 3 goes, whisking after each addition, until a silky-smooth batter forms. Pour this into the prepared traybake tin, level the surface and sprinkle with sesame seeds.

4. Bake for 40–45 minutes until golden brown and slightly crispy on top. Slice up and serve while still warm.

LEMONÓPITA

Lemon Filo Cake

Bursting with vibrant flavour from the juice and zest, *lemonópita* is a lemon version of its more famous orange counterpart, *portokalópita* (see variation on page 196). As with most Greek cakes, *lemonópita* is drenched in a simple cinnamon-infused syrup, so it's incredibly moist and tender. Unlike other recipes, I prepare this without drying out the filo pastry – I go straight in with shredding it up, which I find gives the cake an even more gooey, melt-in-your-mouth texture – and it makes the preparation a lot simpler. I've given the recipe here a little fruity twist by swirling mashed raspberries into the batter. The pop of pink looks beautiful, and the tartness of the raspberries balances the sweetness of this divine cake.

SERVES 16

200g (7oz) caster sugar
200ml (7fl oz) vegetable oil
2 large eggs
zest of 2 lemons and juice of 3
150g (5½oz) Greek yogurt (0% fat)
300g (10½oz) filo pastry (about 10–12 sheets)
1 heaped teaspoon baking powder
1 teaspoon vanilla extract
225g (8oz) raspberries, mashed

For the syrup

275g (9¾oz) caster sugar
175ml (6fl oz) water
1 cinnamon stick

1 Preheat the oven to 170°C fan (375°F), Gas Mark 5 and lightly oil a 23cm (9 inch) square baking dish.

2 First, prepare the syrup. Put the ingredients in a saucepan and place over a high heat. Stir continuously and allow to come to the boil. Once it starts to bubble, take off the heat, remove the cinnamon stick and set aside to cool completely.

3 Meanwhile, whisk together the sugar, oil and eggs in a large bowl until combined. Add the lemon zest, juice and yogurt, and whisk again.

4 Shred the filo pastry into a separate bowl by tearing it with your hands, leaving you with small shavings. Add this to the batter, along with the baking powder and vanilla extract, and stir to combine.

5 Put the raspberries in the bowl you used to shred the pastry. Using the back of a fork, roughly mash the berries to a paste-like consistency.

6 Pour the mixture into the baking dish and drop dollops of the mashed raspberries over the surface. I then swirl the berries through the mixture with a wooden skewer. Bake for 45 minutes until the cake is firm and golden brown on top.

7 Once the cake is cooked, remove it from the oven and carefully pour over the syrup. I use a ladle, pouring over the syrup in several goes, and wait for it to be absorbed before pouring over the next.

8 Leave the cake to cool for at least an hour until it reaches room temperature then place in the fridge to chill for another 3–4 hours: it's key to let the cake chill in the dish before slicing, so that it slices properly.

VARIATION: PORTOKALÓPITA

Orange Filo Cake

This cake is what catapulted my *Eat Like a Greek* series to prominence on social media, with hundreds of thousands of followers saving the recipe and many trying it – only to discover their new-found favourite dessert. You have to give this a go!

Simply use the same ingredients listed for *lemonópita*, substituting the lemon with the zest and juice of 2 oranges, and omitting the raspberries. The steps in the method are the same, except for mashing then swirling in the raspberries.

GALATOMPOÚREKO

Syrupy Filo Custard Pie

Galatompoúreko, or *galaktoboureko*, is a decadent dessert that is typically enjoyed during the Orthodox Easter in both Greece and Cyprus. It has a custard filling sandwiched between layers of filo pastry. It's golden and crispy on top, irresistibly creamy in the middle and drenched in syrup. It can be served either warm or chilled, but I prefer to leave it to cool properly, as this ensures perfect slices. It's a showstopper of a dessert, perfect for dinner parties.

SERVES 12

500ml (18fl oz) full-fat milk
50g (1¾oz) butter
1 teaspoon vanilla extract
120g (4oz) fine semolina, plus extra for dusting
150g (5½oz) caster sugar
2 eggs
10 filo pastry sheets
60–70g (2¼–2½oz) butter, melted

For the syrup

400g (14oz) caster sugar
250ml (9fl oz) water
1 cinnamon stick
squeeze of lemon juice

1 Preheat the oven to 170°C fan (375°F), Gas Mark 5. Prepare a 25 × 32cm (10 × 12½ inch) baking dish by greasing it with butter and lightly dusting with semolina.

2 First, prepare the syrup. Put the ingredients in a saucepan and place over a high heat. Stir continuously and allow to come to the boil. Once it starts to bubble, take off the heat, remove the cinnamon stick and set aside to cool completely.

3 Meanwhile, add the milk, butter and vanilla to a saucepan, place over a medium heat and melt the butter, stirring regularly. Once the butter has melted, add the semolina and stir for 2 minutes until it thickens. Remove the pan from the heat.

4 Whisk together the sugar and eggs in a bowl until frothy. Slowly incorporate this into the pan of custard while continuously stirring over a low heat until it reaches a thick, glossy consistency. Set aside.

5 Line the baking dish with 5 sheets of filo pastry, brushing each with melted butter.

6 Add the custard filling and smooth over evenly. Fold the sides of the pastry sheets in to sit on top of the custard. Top with the remaining 5 sheets of filo pastry, brushing melted butter on each sheet as you go. Slice the *galatompoúreko* into 16 pieces while still in the dish and then bake for 40–45 minutes until golden.

7 Once baked, remove the *galatompoúreko* from the oven and then carefully pour over the syrup – I use a ladle, pouring over the syrup in several goes, and wait for it to be absorbed before pouring over the next. Serve immediately or leave to cool for at least 3 hours. Once completely chilled, the *galatompoúreko* will keep, covered, in the fridge for up to 5 days.

GALATÓPITA

Crustless Custard Pie

Galatópita can be thought of as a creamy, much lighter version of *galaktompoúreko* (see page 198), the baked custard dessert that is popular across the Levant, Turkey and the Balkans as well as in Greece and Cyprus. *Galatópita* is crustless, contains far less sugar, yet it is equally delicious. The core ingredients are milk, semolina and eggs and, once baked, it's drizzled with honey then sprinkled with cinnamon for a stunning finish. What I love about *galatópita* is how simple and straightforward it is to make; a fuss-free and impressive dessert that you can prep in less than 10 minutes.

SERVES 16

1.2 litres (2 pints) full-fat milk
250g (9oz) caster sugar
3 eggs
150g (5½oz) semolina, plus extra for dusting
zest of ½ lemon
100g (3½oz) butter, plus extra for greasing
1 teaspoon vanilla extract

To finish
runny honey
ground cinnamon

1 Preheat the oven to 180°C fan (400°F), Gas Mark 6. Prepare a baking dish (mine is 23cm/9 inches square) by greasing it with butter and lightly dusting with semolina. Add the milk and sugar to a saucepan, place over a medium heat and leave to warm through for 5 minutes, stirring frequently.

2 Meanwhile, whisk together the eggs, semolina and lemon zest in a heatproof bowl. Slowly pour the hot milk into the mixture, whisking continuously until the milk is incorporated.

3 Pour the mixture back into the pan and add the butter and vanilla. Whisking continuously over a medium heat, cook the custard until it thickens (the consistency should be like béchamel). Remove the pan from the heat.

4 Pour the custard into the prepared baking dish and bake for 45 minutes until golden on top.

5 Leave the *galatópita* to cool for an hour before transferring to the fridge and chilling for a further 2 hours before slicing and tucking in. Serve with a drizzle of honey and sprinkle of cinnamon.

6 Store the *galatópita*, covered, in the fridge for up to 4 days.

ELLINIKÓ TSEÏSKÉIK

Greek Yogurt Cheesecake

If you're a fan of cheesecakes, this Greek yogurt-based cheesecake is going to tick all your boxes. It's rich, creamy and slightly tangy from the yogurt-laden filling. The gingernut biscuit base cuts through the richness of the filling and has a subtly spicy kick. Once chilled, I love to top this with a drizzle of honey for extra sweetness, but it's equally delicious served as it is.

SERVES 12

150g (5½oz) butter, melted

300g (10½oz) gingernut biscuits, roughly crushed

1kg (2lb 4oz) Greek yogurt (10% fat)

300g (10½oz) caster sugar

1 teaspoon vanilla extract

6 eggs

runny honey, for drizzling (optional)

1 Preheat the oven to 150°C fan (345°F), Gas Mark 3½ and brush a little melted butter over the base and sides of a 23cm (9 inch) nonstick springform cake tin.

2 To make the biscuit base, put the gingernut biscuits in a food processor and blitz for 10–15 seconds to a fine crumb. Pour in the rest of the melted butter and blitz for another 10–15 seconds to bind the crumbs. Tip the mixture into the greased tin and spread it over the base, pressing down firmly with the back of a spoon to form an even layer and bake for 20 minutes. Remove from the oven and set the tin aside for the biscuit layer to cool for 30 minutes – this will prevent a soggy base.

3 Meanwhile, prepare the filling. Put the yogurt, sugar and vanilla extract in a large mixing bowl (if whisking with a handheld electric whisk) or use a stand mixer with the whisk attachment. Whisk on high speed for 2 minutes until the consistency is fluffy. Then add each egg, one by one, continuing to whisk on high speed for at least 1 minute before adding the next egg. The consistency will be thick and creamy.

4 Pour the filling over the cooled biscuit base and spread evenly. Bake the cheesecake for 1 hour until lightly golden brown.

5 Allow the cheesecake to cool in the tin for at least 1 hour before refrigerating. I recommend keeping it overnight and removing it from the tin the next day, but if you're pressed for time, refrigerate it for at least 3 hours before slicing and serving. If you like, top each portion with a drizzle of runny honey.

6 Store the cheesecake in the fridge in an airtight container and eat within 2 days.

MELÓPITA

Honey Cheesecake

Melópita is a regional speciality of the Greek island of Sifnos. *Méli* means honey and, on the island, this dessert would be made using the local thyme honey. It's a crustless cheesecake and typically contains soft, creamy mizithra (also known as *anthótyros*), a whey cheese made from sheep or goats' milk, notably in Crete. But since this cheese is hard to find outside Greece, I use ricotta cheese here to give an equally creamy texture. I love to add lemon zest for zing, but this is optional. Do choose a good-quality honey as it will make all the difference.

SERVES 8

500g (1lb 2oz) ricotta cheese

200g (7oz) good-quality runny honey

3 large eggs

1½ teaspoons ground cinnamon

1 teaspoon vanilla extract

zest of ½ lemon (optional)

1 Preheat the oven to 160°C fan (350°F), Gas Mark 4. Line a 23cm (9 inch) springform cake tin with baking paper. Put the ricotta in a large mixing bowl and whisk for 1 minute until creamy.

2 Add half the amount of honey to the bowl, along with 1 egg, and whisk again. Then add the second egg and whisk again before adding the third egg and giving everything a final whisk.

3 Stir through half the amount of ground cinnamon along with the vanilla extract and lemon zest (if using).

4 Pour the cheesecake mixture into the lined tin and bake for 1 hour then increase the temperature to 180°C fan (400°F), Gas Mark 6 and bake for 10 minutes more to give it a golden top.

5 Meanwhile, prepare a syrup by putting the remaining honey and cinnamon in a saucepan. Place over a medium heat and leave for a few minutes to infuse. Remove from the heat.

6 Once the cheesecake is baked, allow it to rest for 5–10 minutes before unmoulding from the tin. Place the cheesecake on a serving plate and carefully pour the honey on top. You can serve *melópita* warm or cold, depending on your preference. It keeps in the fridge for up to 3 days in an airtight container.

MILÓPITA

Apple Cake

What is there not to love about a warming, spiced apple cake with a tender crumb? *Milópita* is exactly that: chunks of apple swirled in a tangy, yet caramelized batter that is spiced with cinnamon and nutmeg and topped with more apple, then baked until golden brown. It's perfect served on its own or with a healthy amount of custard.

SERVES 12–16

6 Granny Smith apples

250g (9oz) light brown sugar

2 teaspoons ground cinnamon

3 large eggs

200g (7oz) butter, melted, plus extra for greasing

135g (4¾oz) Greek yogurt (10% fat)

1 teaspoon vanilla extract

400g (14oz) plain flour

1 teaspoon baking powder

½ teaspoon grated nutmeg

1 Preheat the oven to 180°C fan (400°F), Gas Mark 6 and line a 23cm (9 inch) springform cake tin with baking paper. Prepare the apples by first peeling and coring them. Roughly chop 4 into chunks, then put them in a bowl. Cut the remaining 2 apples into quarters then thinly slice each quarter into crescents: these are for the topping. Put them in a separate bowl and sprinkle with 50g (1¾oz) of the sugar and ½ teaspoon of the cinnamon. Mix to coat the slices and set aside.

2 In a large mixing bowl, whisk together the remaining sugar with the eggs, melted butter, Greek yogurt and vanilla extract to a smooth consistency. Then add the dry ingredients, including the remaining 1½ teaspoons of cinnamon, and whisk until a batter forms. Stir through the apple chunks using a spatula, making sure they are well incorporated.

3 Pour the batter into the lined cake tin and level the surface. Top with the sliced apples, arranging them however you like. Bake for 1 hour, or until the cake is firm and golden brown.

4 Leave the cake to cool in the tin for an hour or so before unmoulding. Serve in slices with, if you wish, a dusting of icing sugar or with warm custard.

5 Store in an airtight container and eat within 2 days.

AMYGDALÓPITA

Syrupy Almond Cake

Amygdalópita is the Greek name for a flourless cake soaked in a fragrant syrup infused with brandy, cinnamon and lemon. The cake itself is soft and moist from a combination of ground almonds and panko breadcrumbs. It tastes similar to a frangipane, thanks to the almond extract in the batter, and can be enjoyed as a sweet treat with a cup of tea or as a moreish dessert – it tastes even better once it's been chilled in the fridge, so you can indulge in a slice days after!

SERVES 20–24

200g (7oz) caster sugar

5 eggs

1 teaspoon ground cinnamon

200g (7oz) butter, melted, plus extra for greasing

1 teaspoon almond extract

150g (5½oz) ground almonds

100g (3½oz) panko breadcrumbs

1 teaspoon baking powder

For the syrup

400g (14oz) caster sugar

250ml (9fl oz) water

1 cinnamon stick

1 tablespoon brandy

juice of ½ lemon

1. Preheat the oven to 180°C fan (400°F), Gas Mark 6 and lightly grease a 32 × 22cm (12½ × 8½ inch) traybake tin.

2. First prepare the syrup. Put the ingredients in a saucepan and place over a high heat. Stir continuously and allow to come to the boil. Once it starts to bubble, take off the heat, remove the cinnamon stick and set aside to cool completely.

3. For the cake, put the sugar, eggs and cinnamon in a large mixing bowl (or a stand mixer with the whisk attachment). Beat for 5 minutes then add the melted butter and almond extract and beat for a further 5 minutes until the mixture is light and frothy.

4. Tip in the ground almonds, panko breadcrumbs and baking powder and beat for a final minute until fully incorporated.

5. Pour the batter into the prepared tin and smooth with a spatula to ensure it is spread evenly. Bake for 35 minutes.

6. Once the cake is golden, remove from the oven and poke holes over the surface with a wooden skewer (this will allow the syrup to soak in). Using a ladle, pour over the syrup in several goes, waiting for it to be absorbed into the cake before pouring over the next.

7. Leave the cake to cool for at least an hour until it reaches room temperature, then place in the fridge to chill for another 3–4 hours before slicing and serving. It keeps for up to 3 days in the fridge in an airtight container.

INDOKARIDÓPITA

Syrup-soaked Coconut Cake

Indokaridópita is a lesser-known example of a Greek *siropiastá* (meaning syrup-soaked) cake. Soaked in a zesty syrup and covered in desiccated coconut, this is moist, spongy and light. It's a true crowd-pleaser!

SERVES 24

175g (6½oz) Greek yogurt (10% fat)
200g (7oz) butter, melted, plus extra for greasing
5 eggs, separated
1 teaspoon vanilla extract
250g (9oz) plain flour
250g (9oz) desiccated coconut, plus 75g (2½oz) to decorate
1 teaspoon baking powder
260g (9½oz) caster sugar

For the syrup

400g (14oz) caster sugar
250ml (9fl oz) water
zest of ½ lemon
1 cinnamon stick

1 Preheat the oven to 180°C fan (400°F), Gas Mark 6 and generously grease a 32 × 22cm (12½ × 8½ inch) traybake tin.

2 First prepare the syrup. Put the ingredients in a saucepan and place over a high heat. Stir continuously and allow to come to the boil. Once it starts to bubble, take off the heat, remove the cinnamon stick and set aside to cool completely.

3 To make the cake, combine the Greek yogurt, melted butter, egg yolks and vanilla extract in a large mixing bowl and whisk until smooth. Add the flour, desiccated coconut and baking powder and whisk again to combine.

4 Put the egg whites and caster sugar in a separate bowl and use a handheld electric whisk (or use a stand mixer), and whisk on high speed for 5 minutes until the whites becomes frothy. Pour the mixture into the cake batter and whisk again to incorporate well.

5 Pour the batter into the prepared tin and smooth with a spatula to ensure it is spread evenly. Bake for 40–45 minutes, or until the cake is golden on top and cooked through (check by poking the point of a knife into the centre and see if it comes out clean).

6 Remove the cake from the oven and poke holes over the surface with a wooden skewer to allow the syrup to soak in. Using a ladle, pour over the syrup in several goes, waiting for it to be absorbed into the cake before pouring over the next.

7 Leave the cake to cool for at least 30 minutes before decorating the top with desiccated coconut. Cut into slices – I do this while still in the tin. The cake keeps for up to 3 days in the fridge in an airtight container.

VASILÓPITA

St Basil's Cake

It's traditional in Greece to serve *vasilópita* on the 1st of January in celebration of both the new year and to mark St Basil's Day. This cake recalls how St Basil, known for his care of the poor, baked a cake containing hidden treasures for his people during a famine. *Vasilópita* is traditionally baked with a coin wrapped in foil or baking paper and popped into the cake batter. Whoever receives the slice with the coin is said to have good luck for the rest of the year. The cake itself is beautifully fluffy in texture, as well as zesty and aromatic from the orange zest and blend of spices: mahlepi is an aromatic spice made from ground cherry kernels, while mastic is made from resin of the chia tree and looks a bit like yellow crystals. They both add a unique aroma to the cake and can be sourced from Middle Eastern stores. If you can't find them, ground cardamom works well too.

SERVES 8

250g (9oz) butter, softened, plus extra for greasing
250g (9oz) caster sugar
4 eggs
400g (14oz) self-raising flour
1 teaspoon ground mahlepi
1 teaspoon ground mastic
¼ teaspoon grated nutmeg
1 teaspoon ground cinnamon
100ml (3½fl oz) full-fat milk
zest of 1 orange
icing sugar, for sifting

1. Preheat the oven to 170°C fan (375°F), Gas Mark 5. Grease a 25cm (10 inch) springform cake tin. Put the butter and sugar in a bowl and beat with a handheld electric whisk (or use a stand mixer) for 5 minutes until light and fluffy. Add the eggs, one at a time, beating for about 30 seconds before adding the next one. Continue to beat for another 2 minutes until fluffy.

2. In a separate bowl, add the flour and spices and stir through until roughly incorporated. Then, in 2 goes, add the dry ingredients to the wet mixture. While whisking in the second addition, pour in the milk and continue whisking until the batter is silky and smooth. Fold in the orange zest until it's incorporated.

3. Pour the batter into the prepared cake tin.

4. If you'd like to follow the *vasilópita* tradition, wrap up a coin first in foil, then in baking paper, and pop it into the batter, making sure that it's out of sight.

5. Bake for 1¼ hours until the cake has cooked through (check by inserting a skewer or cocktail stick into the centre – it should come out clean).

6. Leave the cake to cool for 10 minutes in the tin before unmoulding. Liberally sift icing sugar over the top before serving in slices.

SWEET TREATS LIKE A GREEK

Baklava

I love everything that baklava offers: rich, aromatic nuts sandwiched between layers of buttery filo pastry, baked until perfectly golden, and soaked in a simple syrup. This dessert has been made for many centuries and across many different cultures, meaning there is wide variation, ranging from the types of nuts and spices used in the baklava layers, to the ornate shapes in which the filo pastry is crafted. The Greek version is typically made with crushed walnuts, infused with cinnamon and cloves, and soaked in a citrussy syrup. For this, I'm using my foolproof syrup recipe with proportionately less sugar and water, which works perfectly here.

SERVES 20

400g (14oz) walnuts
2 teaspoons ground cinnamon
¼ teaspoon ground cloves
200g (7oz) butter, melted
400g (14oz) filo pastry (about 14–15 sheets)

For the syrup

350g (12oz) caster sugar
260ml (9fl oz) water
3 strips of orange peel
1 cinnamon stick

1 First prepare the syrup. Put the ingredients in a saucepan and place over a high heat. Stir continuously and allow to come to the boil. Once it starts to bubble, take off the heat, remove the orange peel and cinnamon stick and set aside to cool completely.

2 Put the walnuts in a food processor and blitz for 10–15 seconds until they resemble breadcrumbs. Transfer them to a large mixing bowl and stir through the cinnamon and cloves to combine.

3 Preheat the oven to 150°C fan (345°F), Gas Mark 3½. Brush the base and sides of a 25 × 32cm (10 × 12½ inch) baking dish with a little of the melted butter. Lay out the filo pastry sheets on the worktop. Place the first sheet in the dish, letting the ends hang over the edges. Gently press the corners and lightly trickle over 4–5 drizzles of the melted butter, covering the whole sheet. Repeat with a second sheet of filo. This time, fold in the overhanging pastry and gently brush the corners with melted butter.

4 Sprinkle about a fifth of the crushed walnuts over the filo. Continue this layering process another 3–4 times, until all the filling has been used, finishing with 2–3 sheets of filo for the top of the baklava.

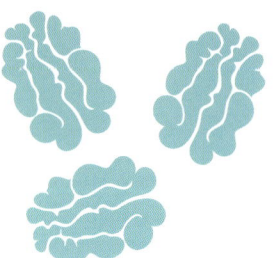

»

5 Once the top sheets are in place, tuck in the sides with the brush, and drizzle any remaining melted butter on top. This time, brush the remaining melted butter all over the top. Place the dish in the fridge to chill for 30 minutes.

6 Once chilled, carefully score the top with a sharp knife into square or diamond shapes without cutting too deeply into the pastry layers. Bake the baklava for 1 hour 10 minutes or until it's golden on top, covering in foil for the final 10 minutes if it becomes golden earlier than that.

7 Once the baklava is cooked, remove from the oven and immediately pour over the syrup. Use a ladle to pour the syrup in several goes, and wait for it to be absorbed into the pastry before pouring over the next.

8 Allow the baklava to cool for at least 1 hour before serving. Cut it into pieces and enjoy fresh on the day, or store in an airtight container to enjoy within 2 days.

KARYDÓPITA

Greek Walnut Cake

This deliciously nutty cake, known as *karydópita* in Greek, is gorgeously moist from being syrup-soaked, yet with the sweetness balanced by spicy flavours. Made with crushed walnuts and a blend of spices, the cake is prepared in two parts: the wet ingredients, which are whipped to form soft peaks, giving the cake its light and spongy texture, and the dry ingredients, which are gently incorporated after. Once the cake is baked to golden-brown perfection, the syrup is poured in batches, and all that's left to do is to slice the cake up and enjoy it!

SERVES 18

For the syrup
325g (11½oz) caster sugar
200ml (7fl oz) water
1 cinnamon stick
2–3 strips of orange peel

For the cake
4 eggs
150g (5½oz) caster sugar
150g (5½oz) butter, melted, plus extra for greasing
225g (8oz) plain flour
1½ teaspoons ground cinnamon
½ teaspoon grated nutmeg
¼ teaspoon ground cloves
1 teaspoon baking powder
300g (10½oz) walnuts, crushed

1. Preheat the oven to 170°C fan (375°F), Gas Mark 5 and generously grease a 32 × 22cm (12½ × 8½ inch) traybake tin.

2. First prepare the syrup. Put the ingredients in a saucepan and place over a high heat. Stir continuously. Once it comes to the boil, take off the heat, remove the orange peel and cinnamon stick and set aside to cool completely.

3. To make the cake, put the eggs and sugar in a stand mixer with the whisk attachment. Beat on a high speed for 5 minutes until the mixture forms soft peaks then add the melted butter and beat on a low speed for a further minute until the mixture is light and frothy.

4. Put all the dry ingredients in another large bowl and stir to combine. Then, in 2 goes, add the dry ingredients to the wet mixture, whisking on a low speed for about 30 seconds each time, until incorporated.

5. Pour the batter into the prepared cake tin and bake for 40 minutes until golden brown and the cake is cooked through (check by inserting a skewer or cocktail stick into the centre – it should come out clean).

6. Remove the cake from the oven and poke holes over the surface with a wooden skewer (this will allow the syrup to soak in). Using a ladle, pour over the syrup in several goes, waiting for it to be absorbed before pouring over the next.

7. Slice the cake and enjoy it warm or chilled. It keeps for up to 3 days in the fridge in an airtight container.

RIZÓGALO

Greek-style Rice Pudding

Greek rice pudding, which is traditionally boiled with a cinnamon stick and cloves and served with a dusting of ground cinnamon on top, is a much-enjoyed dessert. This creamy and delightfully aromatic version uses both single cream and full-fat milk, with less water in the ratio, to make the pudding even more luxurious. To add my own twist, I also add ground cardamom into the mix for an even punchier spice flavour, and swap out the sugar for runny honey for a delicately sweet taste. I love to serve my *rizógalo* with chopped walnuts on top for crunch, but this is totally optional.

SERVES 4

225g (8oz) long-grain rice
270ml (9½fl oz) water
568ml (1 pint) full-fat milk
300ml (10fl oz) single cream
100g (3½oz) runny honey
1 cinnamon stick
4 cloves
½ teaspoon ground cardamon

To serve

ground cinnamon
50g (1¾oz) walnuts, chopped (optional)

1. Wash the rice, rinsing until the water runs clear, then drain and add to a large saucepan, along with the water, milk, cream, honey and spices. Mix well to combine the honey and spices and place the pan over a medium heat. Cook for 35 minutes, uncovered, stirring every 5 minutes or so, or whenever the milk froths, and remove any curdled bits that rise to the top.

2. Once the rice has cooked and the liquid has reduced, remove from the heat, put a lid on the pan and allow the rice pudding to settle for 10 minutes. This will further thicken its consistency.

3. Serve the pudding straight away while it's still warm or leave it to chill in the fridge. Top each portion with a light dusting of ground cinnamon and, if you wish, chopped walnuts for crunch and texture.

PASTAFRÓLA

Apricot Jam Tart

Because this is my mum's favourite Greek dessert, it was a no-brainer that it would feature in my book. *Pastafróla* is a sweet tart made with a shortcrust pastry base, and topped with apricot jam, perfect for satisfying those post-dinner dessert cravings. My shortcrust pastry recipe, which I've used time and time again for mince pies, requires no equipment to make it, just a few staple ingredients. To present *pastafróla* in the time-honoured way, I create a pretty lattice pattern for the top.

SERVES 10–12

160g (5¾oz) margarine, cubed

80g (3oz) caster sugar

320g (11½oz) plain flour, plus extra for dusting

1 teaspoon vanilla extract

1 egg

pinch of salt

350g (12oz) apricot jam

1 To prepare the shortcrust pastry, combine the margarine, sugar, flour and vanilla extract in a large mixing bowl. Rub the ingredients together using your fingertips until the mixture resembles fine breadcrumbs. Then add the egg and salt and fold through the dry ingredients until a dough forms.

2 Cut a third off the dough and set this aside for later. Shape the rest of the dough into a ball and place in a 23cm (9 inch) loose-bottomed flan tin. Use the palms of your hands to begin to flatten the dough, pressing the edges against the sides of the tin to form a pastry shell. To level the base, I like to dust the bottom of a measuring cup with flour and lightly press it down all over the dough until it's completely smooth and even. Then place the pastry-lined tin, along with the remaining third of the dough, in the fridge to chill for 30 minutes. Meanwhile, preheat the oven to 180°C fan (400°F), Gas Mark 6.

3 Once the pastry has chilled, gently spread the apricot jam on top. On a lightly floured surface, roll out the remaining dough as thinly as possible. I like to roll it into a rectangle a little larger than the tin diameter and then slice it into 1cm (½ inch) strips. Slice as many strips that you can from the rolled-out dough and lay these over the filled tart to form a lattice pattern. Trim off any overhanging bits of pastry, roll them into a ball then roll and cut into strips as before. Repeat this process until the lattice top is complete.

4 Bake for 35–40 minutes until the pastry is lightly golden on top. Allow to cool for at least 1 hour before removing from the tin. Serve the *pastafróla* warm or at room temperature. Stored in an airtight container it will keep for up to 3 days.

GIAOÚRTI ME PSITÉS FRÁOULES

Greek-style Yogurt with Roasted Strawberries

Nothing beats a simple yogurt pot for a sweet pick-me-up. Here, the sweetness comes from roasted strawberries caramelized in balsamic vinegar and honey and topped with fresh mint. It's easy to whip up, a healthier alternative to macerating strawberries in sugar and pairs beautifully with Greek yogurt.

SERVES 4

450g (1lb) strawberries, hulled and quartered

2 tablespoons balsamic vinegar

2 tablespoons runny honey

pinch of salt

500g (1lb 2oz) Greek yogurt (10% fat)

4–5 mint leaves, finely chopped

1. Preheat the oven to 200°C fan (425°F), Gas Mark 7. Put the strawberries in an ovenproof dish.

2. Mix together the balsamic vinegar, honey and salt in a small bowl until well combined. Pour this over the strawberries, tossing them well to make sure they are coated evenly.

3. Roast for 15 minutes until the strawberries have softened and caramelized. Leave them to cool for at least 30 minutes to let them set.

4. Divide the yogurt between 4 bowls, top with the roasted strawberries and sprinkle with the chopped mint.

ELLINIKÓS CHALVÁS

Halva

So many countries across the Mediterranean, Middle East, North Africa and parts of Asia have their own take on halva. The word itself derives from the Arabic term *halwā*, meaning sweet. This version, often described in Greece as a semolina pudding, is unbelievably tender and moist, thanks to the use of oil (which also means it is dairy-free and vegan). I use a combination of fine and coarse semolina to give the halva a pleasantly grainy texture, but it's okay to use just fine semolina if that's all that is available to you. Walnuts and semolina are toasted until fragrant before being cooked in a pan with the rest of the ingredients to make a thick paste, which is pressed into a mould and chilled. The result is a nutty no-bake dessert, perfect as a sweet treat with coffee.

SERVES 20

150ml (5fl oz) vegetable oil, plus extra for greasing

100g (3½oz) walnuts, roughly chopped

150g (5½oz) fine semolina

150g (5½oz) coarse semolina

450g (1lb) caster sugar

600ml (20fl oz) water

zest of 1 orange

1½ teaspoons ground cinnamon

¼ teaspoon ground cloves

1 Preheat the oven to 170°C fan (375°F), Gas Mark 5 and grease a 24cm (9½ inch) bundt tin with a teaspoon of oil.

2 Spread out the walnuts in a baking tray and roast for 10 minutes until fragrant. Meanwhile, add the vegetable oil and fine and coarse semolina to a large saucepan. Place it over a medium heat and cook for 10–12 minutes, stirring regularly, until fragrant and lightly golden. Once it becomes a pale, biscuity colour, add the remaining ingredients. Continue to cook, stirring regularly, for another 12–15 minutes until the mix becomes solidified but still malleable.

3 Tip the cooked semolina into the bundt tin, pressing firmly to ensure there are no gaps. This will give the halva its nice shape. Leave the halva to cool for 30–45 minutes at room temperature before refrigerating for at least 3 hours or preferably overnight.

4 Once it has chilled completely, carefully run an offset spatula or blunt knife around the edges of the tin to loosen the halva, then place a large plate on top. Holding both tightly together, flip the halva over on to the plate. Tap the bottom of the tin then carefully lift it off the halva.

5 Slice into about 20 pieces and serve chilled. The halva keeps in the fridge in an airtight container for 3 days.

Greek
St

aples

8.
Greek
Staple

This is my collection of family favourites, recipes that have been passed down the generations. I've included staples that I grew up loving and will always find in the homes of relatives I visit, like my *yiayiá*'s (grandma's) **watermelon jam** and **homemade lemonade**. Both are gorgeously refreshing and simple to make. I've also included **toursí** – Greek-style homemade pickles, which are an essential item in many Greek kitchens and served as an excellent accompaniment to any mezze spread. With a few staples in your cupboard or fridge you really can eat like a Greek!

SPITIKÍ LEMONADÁ

Homemade Lemonade

There's no better way to quench your thirst on a hot summer's day than with a refreshing, lemony drink. And it's even tastier when it's homemade. This recipe is a favourite, enjoyed by my extended family in Cyprus for generations, and I'm sure it will become a household staple for you once you've made a bottle.

MAKES 750ML (1⅓ PINTS)

400g (14oz) caster sugar

500ml (18fl oz) freshly squeezed lemon juice (you will need about 10–14 lemons)

still or sparkling water, to serve

1 Sterilize a 1-litre (1¾-pint) glass bottle by filling it with just-boiled water. After 10 minutes, carefully empty the bottle and allow to return to room temperature.

2 Meanwhile, add the sugar and freshly squeezed lemon juice to a large bowl and stir well until the sugar has dissolved.

3 Place a funnel in the top of the bottle. Using a ladle, carefully pour in the lemonade. Seal the bottle and store it in the fridge for up to a month.

4 To serve, mix 50ml (2fl oz) of the lemonade – more if you prefer it sweeter – with 250ml (9fl oz) of still or sparkling water. Enjoy chilled.

MARMELÁDA KARPOÚZI

Watermelon Jam

If you've never tried watermelon jam before, let this be a sign. Try making this using the rind next time you are enjoying the sweet flesh – once blitzed up and simmered with sugar, the rind turns into a gorgeous refreshing jam. It's delightful spread on warm, buttery toast.

MAKES 1 × 340G (11¾OZ) JAR

half a watermelon
100g (3½oz) caster sugar

1 Start by peeling off and discarding the thin green skin from the watermelon (it's easiest to do this before cutting it up). Next, cut the watermelon half in two and scoop out or cut off the pink flesh – set this aside for another recipe (such as the Watermelon and Feta Salad on page 88). Chop the remaining tough white rind into small chunks, then weigh off 400g (14oz) of the pieces. I like to add these to a blender and quickly blitz them until their consistency is mushy – it only needs about 10 seconds.

2 Pour this mushy mixture into a large saucepan and place over a medium heat. Leave it to heat up for 2–3 minutes. When the liquid begins to bubble, add the sugar and stir.

3 The jam will need to cook for a total of 40 minutes. In the first 20 minutes, the rind will reduce and become a pinky-orange colour. Stir the mixture regularly throughout the cooking time to stop it from sticking to the pan.

4 After about 30 minutes, reduce the temperature to low and cook for a further 10 minutes to allow the jam to thicken and solidify. To check that it's set, simply scoop up a bit on the spoon – it should slowly drip back into the pan. Remove the pan from the heat and leave the jam to cool before storing it.

5 Meanwhile, sterilize your jar. Fill it with just-boiled water and leave for 10 minutes before carefully emptying it out and allowing it to return to room temperature. I use a tablespoon to add the jam in batches to avoid it spilling over the sides.

6 Store the jam in the fridge and use it within 2 weeks.

NTRÉSIN'NK SALÁTASE

Greek Salad Dressing

A sexy dressing can take any bog-standard salad to the next level. This Greek-inspired one is versatile and simply delicious. Store in the fridge, ready for use, then shake it up, pour over your salad and enjoy.

SERVES 4–6

100ml (3½fl oz) extra virgin olive oil

3 tablespoons red wine vinegar

1 teaspoon wholegrain mustard

1 teaspoon dried oregano

½ teaspoon salt (or to taste)

1 Start by sterilizing a jam jar. Fill with just-boiled water and leave for 10 minutes before carefully emptying it out and allowing it to return to room temperature.

2 Add all the dressing ingredients to the jar and stir with a spoon to combine. Seal tightly with a lid and refrigerate for up to 3 days. The oil will semi-solidify but returns to liquid once it is at room temperature. Shake before using to recombine the oil and vinegar.

MARINÁDA KRÉATOS

All-purpose Marinade

The key to a good marinade is to include these three components: acid, fat and a combination of herbs and spices. Here, I'm using white wine vinegar as the acid that tenderizes the meat and keeps it juicy and soft. Extra virgin olive oil is my go-to choice of fat, along with crushed garlic and a mix of oregano (*rígani* in Greek) and paprika. It's simple to prepare and versatile – use it for a variety of meats, such as chicken, pork and lamb. You can prep this in advance and store it in the fridge or marinate your meat straight away. The result will be super-tender and delicious meat.

ENOUGH FOR 500G (1LB 2OZ) OF MEAT

generous 3 tablespoons extra virgin olive oil

4 teaspoons white wine vinegar

2 garlic cloves, crushed

1 teaspoon lemon zest

2 teaspoons dried oregano

½ teaspoon smoked paprika

½–1 teaspoon salt, to taste

¼ teaspoon ground black pepper

1 Mix all the ingredients in a non-metallic bowl and add your chosen meat. Turn to coat and leave either overnight or for at least 2 hours.

TOURSÍ

Pickled Vegetables

Toursí is the Greek word for pickled vegetables, and you'll find this fermented delicacy served in Greece as an appetizer on most mezze spreads. Homemade *toursí* is a great way to add flavour and texture to a plate of bread and cheese or a simple salad, and I often enjoy some as a tasty snack to munch on. Making a batch of pickles is super simple – here I've used peppers, carrots, cucumbers and cauliflower, but fennel is also good – plus some whole spices for a kick.

MAKES 2 × 500ML (18FL OZ) JARS

For the brine

400ml (14fl oz) water
200ml (7fl oz) white wine vinegar
2 tablespoons caster sugar
1 tablespoon salt

For the vegetables

1 red pepper, stem and seeds removed, thinly sliced
2 carrots, thinly sliced
4 baby or Lebanese cucumbers, quartered lengthways
½ small cauliflower, cut into small florets

For the spices

6 garlic cloves, thinly sliced
2 teaspoons coriander seeds
2 teaspoons peppercorns
2 teaspoons mustard seeds
4 bay leaves

1 Start by preparing the brine. Combine the water, vinegar, sugar and salt in a large saucepan. Stir, place over a medium heat and bring to the boil. As soon as the mixture begins to bubble, remove the pan from the heat and set the brine aside to cool.

2 Meanwhile, sterilize the jars by filling with just-boiled water. After 10 minutes, carefully empty the jars and allow to return to room temperature.

3 Prepare the vegetables and keep them separate.

4 Place half the quantities of sliced garlic, spices and bay leaves in the base of each jar. Top with the prepped vegetables, dividing them equally between the jars. (I like to start with the longer veg, keeping the pepper strips and cucumber quarters around the edges of the jar, and packing the carrot slices and cauliflower florets in between.)

5 Using a ladle, carefully pour the brine into the jars, ensuring the vegetables are completely covered. Seal with the lids and store in the fridge. Leave the *toursí* to pickle for at least a week before serving. Unopened, the jars will keep for at least 2 months. Once opened, eat within 1 month.

Index

A
all-purpose marinade 231
almonds
　Greek almond cookies 182
　Greek festive shortbread 187
　Greek-style biscotti 178
　syrupy almond cake 207
apple cake 204
apricot jam tart 216
aubergines
　aubergine dip 26
　aubergine filo pie 152–3
　moussaka 147–8
　roasted aubergine salad 74

B
baked meatballs 142–4
baklava 210–12
beans
　cannellini bean soup 102
　Greek baked beans 96
　green bean stew 101
beef
　baked meatballs 142–4
　beef patties 114
　beef patties in gyros form 115
　dolma cake 136–8
　filo meat pie 129
　Greek lasagne 139–41
　Greek meatballs 66
　moussaka 147–8
　orzo stew 107
　slow-cooked beef stew 149
　stuffed onions 124–5
　stuffed peppers and tomatoes 135
beetroot salad 84
biscuits
　chocolate salami 185
　Greek festive shortbread 187
　Greek-style biscotti 178
　white chocolate salami 186
brandy
　chocolate salami 185

Greek festive shortbread 187
bread
　baked meatballs 142–4
　Cypriot pitta bread 58–9
　Cypriot village bread 61–3
　Greek cheese bread 158
　Greek-style panzanella 81
　halloumi bread 160–1
　olive bread 160–1
　taramasalata 31
breadcrumbs
　beef patties 114
　Greek meatballs 66
bulgur wheat
　tomatoey bulgur wheat 110

C
cabbage slaw 77
cakes
　apple cake 204
　Greek walnut cakes 213
　lemon filo cake 195–6
　olive oil cake 192
　orange filo cake 195–6
　St Basil's cake 209
　syrup-soaked coconut cake 208
　syrupy almond cake 207
calamari 64
cannellini bean soup 102
carrots
　chickpea stew 103
　Cypriot-style lentil rice 99
　filo meat pie 129
　Greek baked beans 96
　orzo stew 107
　pickled vegetables 232
celery
　cannellini bean soup 102
　Greek lentil soup 98
cheese
　cheese croquettes with kataïfi 43
　Cypriot cheese pies 173
　Cypriot sweet cheese dumplings 170–1

filo meat pie 129
Greek cheese bread 158
Greek lasagne 139–41
halloumi bread 160–1
kataïfi-crusted pan-fried cheese 46
layered feta and tomato bake 52
moussaka 147–8
orzo stew 107
stovetop tomato orzo 108
thin-battered cheese pie 165
see also feta
cheesecake
　Greek yogurt cheesecake 201
　honey cheesecake 203
chicken
　chicken gyros 133
　Greek lemon chicken 130
　lemony chicken and rice soup 122
chickpeas
　chickpea patties 41
　chickpea salad 87
　chickpea stew 103
　hummus 19
chilli
　baked meatballs 142–4
　layered feta and tomato bake 52
　pan-fried peppers and feta 48
　pan-fried prawns in tomato sauce 113
　slow-cooked beef stew 149
　spicy feta dip 20
chocolate
　chocolate salami 185
　white chocolate salami 186
coconut
　syrup-soaked coconut cake 208
cod roe
　taramasalata 31
cookies
　Greek almond cookies 182
　Greek Easter cookies 174
courgettes
　courgette feta dip 16
　courgette fritters 42

crispy courgette chips 47
tomato fritters 38
cranberries
  white chocolate salami 186
cream
  Greek-style rice pudding 215
crustless custard pie 200
cucumbers
  chickpea salad 87
  Greek village salad 78
  Greek-style orzo salad 76
  pickled vegetables 232
  tzatziki 23
Cypriot cheese pies 173
Cypriot pitta bread 58–9
Cypriot sweet cheese dumplings 170–1
Cypriot tahini pies 181
Cypriot village bread 61–3
Cypriot-style lentil rice 99
Cypriot-style potato salad 73

D
dill
  cabbage slaw 77
  courgette feta dip 16
  Greek lettuce salad 83
  Greek-style spinach risotto 104
  okra stew 109
  tzatziki 23
dolma cake 136–8

E
eggs
  cheese croquettes with kataïfi 43
  courgette fritters 42
  crustless custard pie 200
  Cypriot cheese pies 173
  kataïfi-crusted pan-fried cheese 46
  lemony chicken and rice soup 122
  syrupy filo custard pie 198
  thin-battered cheese pie 165
  tomatoey scrambled eggs with feta 94

F
feta
  aubergine filo pie 152–3
  beetroot salad 84
  chickpea salad 87
  courgette feta dip 16
  courgette fritters 42
  fried feta cheese parcel 51
  Greek baked beans 96
  Greek cheese bread 158
  Greek lettuce salad 83
  Greek-style orzo salad 76
  Greek-style panzanella 81
  Greek-style spinach risotto 104
  Greek village salad 78
  layered feta and tomato bake 52
  pan-fried peppers and feta 48
  pan-fried prawns in tomato sauce 113
  spicy feta dip 20
  spicy honey feta dip 22
  spinach pie filo swirls 166–9
  thin-battered cheese pie 165
  tomatoey scrambled eggs with feta 94
  watermelon with feta 88
  see also cheese
filo pastry
  aubergine filo pie 152–3
  baklava 210–12
  filo meat pie 129
  filo pumpkin pies 180
  fried feta cheese parcel 51
  lemon filo cake 195–6
  orange filo cake 195–6
  spinach pie filo swirls 166–9
  syrupy filo custard pie 198
  see kataïfi
flatbreads
  Cypriot pitta bread 58–9
  Greek flatbreads 57
fried feta cheese parcel 51

G
garlic
  aubergine dip 26
  aubergine filo pie 152–3
  garlicky potato dip 28
  okra stew 109
  pan-fried prawns in tomato sauce 113
  pork gyros 134
  slow-cooked beef stew 149
  split pea dip 27
Greek almond cookies 182
Greek baked beans 96
Greek cheese bread 158
Greek Easter cookies 174
Greek festive shortbread 187
Greek flatbreads 57
Greek lasagne 139–41
Greek lemon chicken 130
Greek lentil soup 98
Greek lettuce salad 83
Greek meatballs 66
Greek salad dressing 230
Greek-style biscotti 178
Greek-style panzanella 81
Greek-style rice pudding 215
Greek-style spinach risotto 104
Greek-style yogurt with roasted strawberries 219
Greek village salad 78
Greek walnut cake 213
Greek yogurt cheesecake 201
green bean stew 101

H
halloumi bread 160–1
halva 220
homemade lemonade 226
honey
  Cypriot tahini pies 181
  fried feta cheese parcel 51
  Greek flatbreads 57
  honey cheesecake 203
  honey sesame bars 177
  spicy honey feta dip 22
hummus 19

J
jam
  apricot jam tart 216
  watermelon jam 229

K
kataïfi (shredded filo)
  cheese croquettes with kataïfi 43
  kataïfi-crusted pan-fried cheese 46

L
lamb
  lamb souvlaki 116
  slow-cooked lamb 150
lasagne, Greek 139–41
layered feta and tomato bake 52
leeks
  spinach pie filo swirls 166–9
lemons
  Greek lemon chicken 130
  Greek-style spinach risotto 104
  homemade lemonade 226
  lemon filo cake 195–6
  lemony chicken and rice soup 122
  lemony roast potatoes 145
  marinated green olives 36
  stuffed vine leaves 55–6
lentils
  Cypriot-style lentil rice 99
  Greek lentil soup 98
lettuce
  Greek lettuce salad 83

M
marinade, all-purpose 231
marinated green olives 36
mint
  beef patties 114
  Cypriot cheese pies 173
  Greek cheese bread 158
  Greek lettuce salad 83
  Greek meatballs 66
  Greek-style spinach risotto 104
  watermelon with feta 88
moussaka 147–8

O
okra stew 109
olive oil
  all-purpose marinade 231
  Greek salad dressing 230

hummus 19
olive oil cake 192
olives
  chickpea salad 87
  Greek village salad 78
  marinated green olives 36
  olive bread 160–1
onions
  aubergine filo pie 152–3
  baked meatballs 142–4
  beef patties 114
  cannellini bean soup 102
  chicken gyros 133
  chickpea patties 41
  chickpea stew 103
  Cypriot-style lentil rice 99
  dolma cake 136–8
  Greek lentil soup 98
  Greek meatballs 66
  green bean stew 101
  pork gyros 134
  slow-cooked lamb 150
  stuffed onions 124–5
  stuffed peppers and tomatoes 135
oranges
  Greek Easter cookies 174
  Greek-style biscotti 178
  halva 220
  orange filo cake 195–6
  St Basil's cake 209
oregano
  Greek lemon chicken 130
  Greek-style panzanella 81
  lemony roast potatoes 145
orzo
  Greek-style orzo salad 76
  orzo stew 107
  stovetop tomato orzo 108

P
pan-fried prawns in tomato sauce 113
parsley
  beef patties 114
  Cypriot-style potato salad 73
pasta
  Greek lasagne 139–41

Greek-style orzo salad 76
orzo stew 107
stovetop tomato orzo 108
tomatoey bulgur wheat 110
peppers
  aubergine dip 26
  aubergine filo pie 152–3
  Greek baked beans 96
  Greek village salad 78
  pan-fried peppers and feta 48
  pickled vegetables 232
  roasted aubergine salad 74
  slow-cooked lamb 150
  spicy feta dip 20
  stuffed peppers and tomatoes 135
pickled vegetables 232
pork
  baked meatballs 142–4
  Greek lasagne 139–41
  Greek meatballs 66
  pork gyros 134
potatoes
  Cypriot-style potato salad 73
  garlicky potato dip 28
  green bean stew 101
  lemony roast potatoes 145
  moussaka 147–8
  okra stew 109
  slow-cooked lamb 150
prawns
  pan-fried prawns in tomato sauce 113
pumpkin
  filo pumpkin pies 180

R
raisins
  Cypriot cheese pies 173
  filo pumpkin pies 180
raspberries
  lemon filo cake 195–6
rice
  Cypriot-style lentil rice 99
  dolma cake 136–8
  Greek-style rice pudding 215
  Greek-style spinach risotto 104
  lemony chicken and rice soup 122

stuffed onions 124–5
stuffed peppers and tomatoes 135
stuffed vine leaves 55–6
roasted aubergine salad 74

S

salads
  beetroot salad 84
  cabbage slaw 77
  chickpea salad 87
  Cypriot-style potato salad 73
  Greek lettuce salad 83
  Greek salad dressing 230
  Greek-style orzo salad 76
  Greek-style panzanella 81
  Greek village salad 78
  roasted aubergine salad 74
seafood
  calamari 64
  pan-fried prawns in tomato sauce 113
semolina
  crispy courgette chips 47
  crustless custard pie 200
  halva 220
  syrupy filo custard pie 198
sesame seeds
  cheese croquettes with kataïfi 43
  Cypriot village bread 61–3
  fried feta cheese parcel 51
  Greek-style biscotti 178
  honey sesame bars 177
shallots
  stuffed vine leaves 55–6
  taramasalata 31
slow-cooked beef stew 149
slow-cooked lamb 150
spicy feta dip 20
spicy honey feta dip 22
spinach
  Greek-style spinach risotto 104
  spinach pie filo swirls 166–9
split pea dip 27
spring onions
  cabbage slaw 77
  courgette fritters 42
  garlicky potato dip 28

Greek lettuce salad 83
halloumi bread 160–1
olive bread 160–1
roasted aubergine salad 74
stuffed vine leaves 55–6
tomato fritters 38
squid
  calamari 64
St Basil's cake 209
strawberries
  Greek-style yogurt with roasted strawberries 219
stuffed onions 124–5
stuffed peppers and tomatoes 135
stuffed vine leaves 55–6
syrup-soaked coconut cake 208
syrupy almond cake 207
syrupy filo custard pie 198

T

tahini
  Cypriot tahini pies 181
  hummus 19
  tahini dip 25
taramasalata 31
thin-battered cheese pie 165
tomatoes
  baked meatballs 142–4
  chickpea salad 87
  dolma cake 136–8
  Greek baked beans 96
  Greek lasagne 139–41
  Greek lentil soup 98
  Greek-style orzo salad 76
  Greek-style panzanella 81
  Greek village salad 78
  green bean stew 101
  layered feta and tomato bake 52
  moussaka 147–8
  okra stew 109
  pan-fried peppers and feta 48
  pan-fried prawns in tomato sauce 113
  slow-cooked beef stew 149
  stovetop tomato orzo 108
  stuffed onions 124–5
  stuffed peppers and tomatoes 135

tomato fritters 38
tomatoey bulgur wheat 110
tomatoey scrambled eggs with feta 94
tzatziki 23

V

vegetables
  pickled vegetables 232
vine leaves
  dolma cake 136–8
  stuffed vine leaves 55–6

W

walnuts
  baklava 210–12
  beetroot salad 84
  filo pumpkin pies 180
  Greek walnut cake 213
  halva 220
  roasted aubergine salad 74
  spicy honey feta dip 22
watermelon jam 229
watermelon with feta 88
white chocolate salami 186
wine
  filo meat pie 129
  Greek lasagne 139–41
  moussaka 147–8

Y

yogurt
  apple cake 204
  beetroot salad 84
  chicken gyros 133
  courgette feta dip 16
  Cypriot pitta bread 58–9
  Greek yogurt cheesecake 201
  Greek-style yogurt with roasted strawberries 219
  lamb souvlaki 116
  lemon filo cake 195–6
  orange filo cake 195–6
  pork gyros 134
  syrup-soaked coconut cake 208
  tzatziki 23

UK/US Terms

UK	US
AUBERGINE	EGGPLANT
BAKING PAPER	PARCHMENT PAPER
BAKING TRAY	BAKING SHEET
BARBECUE	GRILL
BEEF TOMATOES	BEEFSTEAK TOMATOES
BEETROOT	BEET
BICARBONATE OF SODA	BAKING SODA
BUTTER BEANS	LIMA BEANS
CASTER SUGAR	SUPERFINE SUGAR
CELERY STICKS	CELERY STALKS
CHICKPEAS	GARBANZO BEANS
CHIPS	FRIES
CLINGFILM	PLASTIC WRAP
COLANDER	STRAINER
CORIANDER (HERB)	CILANTRO
CORNFLOUR	CORN STARCH
COS LETTUCE	ROMAINE LETTUCE
COURGETTE	ZUCCHINI
FRYING PAN	SKILLET
FULL-FAT MILK	WHOLE MILK
GRILL (N.)	BROILER
GROUND ALMONDS	POWDERED ALMONDS
HOB	STOVETOP
ICING SUGAR	CONFECTIONER'S SUGAR
JAM	JELLY
KITCHEN PAPER	PAPER TOWEL
MINCED BEEF/PORK	GROUND BEEF/PORK
PASSATA	STRAINED TOMATOES
PEPPER	BELL PEPPER
PLAIN FLOUR	ALL-PURPOSE FLOUR
PRAWNS	SHRIMP
ROCKET	ARUGULA
SELF-RAISING FLOUR	SELF-RISING FLOUR
SEMOLINA	FARINA
SIEVE	STRAINER
SINGLE CREAM	LIGHT CREAM
SPRING ONIONS	SCALLIONS
STOCK CUBE	BOUILLON CUBE
TEA TOWEL	DISH TOWEL
TIN	PAN
TOMATO PURÉE	TOMATO PASTE
ZEST	RIND

Acknowledgements

Where do I begin? The list of people to thank is very long, but the only place I know where to start is, of course, by thanking my one and only mum. My rock, my number one cheerleader and beneficiary/guinea pig when it comes to testing out new recipes. You've stood by me through everything and I simply wouldn't be the person I am today without you. I love you to the moon and back.

To my brothers and all my family across the world, thank you for sharing your excitement with me. Your enthusiasm for and pride in my creative ventures keeps me going.

To all my incredible friends – but especially Anna, Rose, Maia, Rachel and Haami. The countless voice notes cheering me on from afar, phone calls to check in and dinners at mine where you tested out my recipes kept me motivated and grounded, even in the most demanding of times. I'm so lucky to have you!

To my talented fellow content creators – Anouchka, Victoria, Daniel, Priyansh, Karen, Jess and Martha. Thank you for cheering me on and celebrating all wins with me – no matter how small. You continue to inspire me with your talent and tenacity.

To Lauren and Callen, my talented literary agents from Bell Lomax. I couldn't have asked for anyone more genuine, sincere and passionate to work with. I still remember our first email exchange back in January 2024. It was thoughtful, and I could tell just how deeply invested you were from the get-go. You believed in my potential even before I recognized it myself. It's been an incredible journey from concept to cookbook creation and, throughout it all, you've guided me at every step of the way. Thank you for instilling hope in me, for clarifying all my doubts and questions at speed and with ease, and for keeping me in check, always.

To everyone at Hamlyn. I'd like to start off by giving my biggest thanks to Kate for taking a chance on me. Thank you for committing to *Eat Like a Greek* and for bringing this dream of mine to life. None of this would have been possible without you.

To Juliette, the loveliest person to have had by my side at the photoshoot. Your artistic direction for the book has been beyond anything I could have ever imagined and I'm deeply grateful for your contributions.

To Leanne and Stephanie, the best editors EVER. Thank you for your thoughtful feedback, scrupulous editing and endless patience as we revised and refined many iterations of the manuscript. Your input has been instrumental in transforming this book into its most authentic and polished version. P.S. I love that you've learned a bit of Greek along the way!

To Andrew, your sheer talent shines through every photograph in this book. Thank you for making me feel so comfortable and so celebrated on set. Working with you to bring *Eat Like a Greek* to life has been such an honour and privilege, and I fondly remember our banter and the copious amount of cake we shared. P.S. thanks for recommending *Stath Lets Flats*!

To Rae, I'm in awe of your photo editing – doing so with such ease even while on the shoot! Thank you for your calming and grounding presence, and for making the whole photoshoot so special.

To Emily and Christine, the most talented food stylists. Working alongside you both has been such a privilege – whether that was witnessing the magic of a dish being brought to life, the slightly frantic moments in the kitchen or just simply enjoying the fruits of our labour over lunch. Thank you for your insights and expertise, and for collaborating with me on making every recipe the best that it could be. I couldn't have asked for anyone better.

To Max, the talented prop stylist. You're the reason I laughed so much on set. Thank you for staging each dish so intentionally and for making the photoshoot such a joy.

Last but not least, to everyone who has been following chefmarinie, thank you from the bottom of my heart for every single like, comment, save and share. You are the reason I've been able to write this cookbook and I'm forever grateful for your support.

About the Author

Marina Georgallides (@chefmarinie) is a Greek-Cypriot London-based food blogger. Her journey into food content creation started in earnest at the beginning of 2021 when she made a promise to herself to post a recipe every single day for a month. She gradually galvanized an audience through her food series, *Just Jamming*, which paved the way for subsequent food series like *Noughties Nostalgia*, *Only Cans* and *Eat Like a Greek*.

chefmarinie
@chefmarinie
@chefmarinie